MARCO POLO

This edition published 2017
By Living Book Press
147 Durren Rd, Jilliby, 2259

ISBN: 978-1-925729-22-1

 A catalogue record for this
book is available from the
National Library of Australia

Marco Polo

HIS TRAVELS AND ADVENTURES

———————

By George Makepeace Towle

LIVING BOOK
PRESS

PREFACE

————————⟨∽⟩————————

HE reader is carried back, in the present volume, to a period two centuries previous to the discovery of the route to India by Vasco da Gama, and to the conquest of Peru by Pizarro. A young Venetian of the thirteenth century, brought up amid luxury and wealth, of a bold spirit and a curious mind, went forth from his home in the beautiful Queen City of the Adriatic, and for many years lived among a far-off Asiatic people, and at a court of barbaric and yet splendid pomp.

He made many far and dangerous journeyings in the wild distant lands and among the fierce tribes of Cathay, Thibet, India, and Abyssinia. His life was passed amid an almost incessant succession of exciting events, of strange adventures, and of hair-breadth escapes. He rose to high distinction and power at the Tartar court of the mighty Kublai Khan, one of the most famous conquerors and potentates who ever, in either ancient or modern times, have led legions to devastating wars, or have ruled teeming millions with despotic sway.

Nor did his career of valor and stirring action end with his return, middle-aged and laden with riches, to his native Venice. He engaged in the bitter warfare between the two rival republics of the sea, Venice and Genoa; became a prisoner of the latter state: and while in prison, dictated the wondrous narrative of his adventures which still survives, a precious legacy left by this great traveller to later generations.

I have attempted to transform the somewhat dry and monotonous translation of this narrative into an entertaining story, that may engage the attention and the interest of my young readers; for which it certainly presents ample opportunities. If the task is properly done, no one can fail to follow Marco Polo from his Venetian home, across the entire continent of Asia to the court of Kublai Khan, and in his various adventures and journeys while in the far-off Orient, without eager curiosity and ever-deepening interest. The central figure of the story is heroic, for Marco Polo was in all things manly, brave, persevering, intelligent, and chivalrous; and the scenes and incidents in which he was the leading actor were in the highest degree thrilling and dramatic.

Contents

MARCO POLO

CHAPTER I.

The Return of the Wanderers

BEAUTIFUL as Venice now is, in the days of its stagnation and decay, it was a yet more beautiful city seven centuries ago. Then its quays and Grand Canal were crowded with the ships of every nation; its bazaars and marts were bustling with active trade, and were picturesque in the mingling of the gay and brilliant costumes of the East, with the more sober attire of the European peoples; its noble and lofty palaces, not yet, as we now see them, hoary and dilapidated, rose in fresh splendor from the verge of its watery and winding streets; the dome of St. Mark's shone with new gilding, and its walls with recent frescoing; the Piazza was nightly crowded with throngs of gallant nobles and cavaliers, long-bearded, prosperous merchants, and bevies of fair dames, whose black veils swept from their fair foreheads to their dainty feet. Venice was not only a queen among commercial cities, but a great warlike power; with brave and well-disciplined armies, hardy captains, formidable fleets, and proud strongholds, where, on either shore of the sparkling Adriatic, she held her own valiantly, against Turk, Austrian, and Genoese. Mighty princes sought the hands of the daughters of Venice in marriage; the Doges who ruled over the stately city were greeted by Emperors and Kings as their brothers and equals; the conquests of Venice reached to Asia and to Africa; her ships rode the purple waters of the Mediterranean in haughty defiance of the galleys of her rivals. Around the patriarchal Doges was gathered a gorgeous court. There were festal days when the Grand Canal, bordered by palaces on either side, was crowded thick with gilded and canopied barges, and interminable lines of gondolas, each gay craft filled with richly attired cavaliers and dames, on whom jewels sparkled, and above whom rose many-colored banners that announced their rank and station: while, after night-fall, the air was alive with the most dazzling fire-works, which fairly hid moon, stars, and the heaven's canopy from view.

It is in Venice, at this period of her greatness and glory, that our story opens.

A mellow, hazy autumn day was drawing to its close. The sky was lit with that soft, rich, yellow sunset glow, which has always been remarked as one of the loveliest sights to be seen at Venice; the last rays of the sun glittered upon the gilded dome of Saint Mark's; the broad square before the ancient cathedral was beginning to fill with its evening multitude of cavaliers and coquettes. In the Grand Canal, and the glassy lagoon beyond, the gondoliers lazily plied their long oars, or rested their gondolas on the still waters. It was an hour in which whatever there was of activity and bustle in Venice, became indolent and tranquil; when men and women sought their ease under a sky which compelled serenity and reverie. In the bazaars, on the Rialto, and the Piazza, the stalls were laden with bunches of large and luscious grapes, with figs of many colors, so ripe that the gummy juice oozed from them, and with pomegranates, upon whose cheeks glowed the rich red bloom which betrayed their full ripeness; and there was scarcely to be seen a Venetian of the lower class, who was not munching some of the succulent fruit which his climate produced in such cheap and varied abundance.

Not far from the centre of the beautiful city, on one of the many canals which serve it instead of streets, stood a lofty mansion, which, at one's first approach, seemed two. Three stories in height, it towered above many of the surrounding buildings: and between its two wings stood an archway, richly decorated with scrolls and figures of animals, surmounted by an ornate cross; while, above the archway, rose a tall square tower. Entering the archway, you would have found yourself in a spacious, paved court-yard, which the house, quadrangular in shape, completely enclosed. The inner walls were adorned, like: the archway, with sculptured devices, among which you might have ob-served a coat-of-arms, comprising a shield, with a wide bar running across it, upon which were graven three birds. The whole mansion was stately and imposing, and betokened that its possessors were at once rich and of high rank.

On the late afternoon which has been described, an unusual bustle was going on in and near this house. It was full of gayly-dressed people, old and young, all of whom were evidently in a state of excitement. Servants hurried to and fro in the corridors; in the pretty balconies which were built at the windows facing the canal of San Giovanni Crisostomo, were gathered groups of cavaliers and ladies, who were leaning over and peering eagerly out to the end of the watery thoroughfare, as if they were anxiously expecting an arrival.

In the main hall of the mansion, a vast apartment, approached from the court-yard by a broad flight of stone steps, and entered by a high and richly-sculptured portal stood a knot of persons who seemed even more excited than the rest. One was a tall and dignified man, clad in a long blue cloak, his head covered by a slashed blue and white cap, from which rose an ostrich feather. He wore a long, brown beard, just streaked with gray; his dark face was flushed, and every moment he approached the door, and questioned the servants posted in the court-yard. On either side of him stood two youths, one fifteen and the other thirteen, both very richly attired, and both the very pictures of boyish freshness and beauty. The elder was tall for his age, and his form was straight, graceful, and well-knit. A pair of bright gray eyes, a nose rather longer than medium, full red lips, and a handsome round chin, comprised his features, the expression of his face was at once energetic and pleasing; his movements were quick and nervous; and every now and then he turned to the cavalier beside him, and talked rapidly in a strong, musical voice. The younger boy, while he closely resembled his brother, was of more gentle mould and manners. The one seemed made to be a warrior, to play an active, perhaps a heroic part, in the struggling world. The other appeared born to be a courtier, to shine in the society of elegant women, to be rather a favorite of the polite world, than a man of deeds. While the younger clung to the cavalier's arm with sort of air of dependence, the elder bore himself erect, as if quite able to take care of himself.

All at once loud and joyous cries were heard from the balconies in front of the house; and presently down rushed their occupants into the hall, whither all the others who were in the house flocked in a twinkling.

"They are coming! They are coming!" were the words that went eagerly around. The two lads were seized and embraced by the ladies; the elder's eyes kindled with delight as he hurried to the door; his brother danced up and down, and clapped his hands, while tears of happiness flowed over his rosy cheeks.

In the court-yard there was the greatest noise and confusion. The retainers of the household gathered in two rows at the archway, while the steward, a portly personage, in a tunic, with a heavy chain around his neck, and a long staff in his hand, passed out upon the landing to welcome the new-comers.

He was soon seen returning, walking backwards, and bowing, as he came, almost to the ground. In another moment the travellers who had been so anxiously awaited, slowly walked through the archway, and greeted the excited group before them.

A strange appearance, indeed, did the two tall, bronzed men present to those who were gazing at them. Instead of the rich and elegant Venetian costume of the day, their forms were covered with what seemed rough and barbarous garments. From their shoulders to their feet they were arrayed in long, loose gowns, or great-coats, one of them made of shaggy fur; while on their heads were fur caps. Their feet were incased in rude shoes, which turned up at the toes; while at their sides, instead of the long, slender Venetian sword, hung broad, heavy, curved scimitars. In their hands they carried stout sticks; slung across their shoulders were long, furry bags. Not less strange were their faces. Both wore long, shaggy, grizzled hair, which fell in thick masses to their shoulders; the beards of both were long and tangled, and covered their cheeks almost to their eyes; their skin was rough and brown, and here and there a seamed scar betokened that they had met with fierce and savage enemies.

No sooner had they appeared than the elder of the two boys pushed his way through the crowd, which parted to let him pass, and rushed up to the new-comers as if to throw himself into the arms of one of them. But when he came close to them, he suddenly stopped short. In place of the light of joy, a puzzled and pained expression came across

RETURN OF THE WANDERERS

his handsome face. He looked, first at one and then at the other; peered into their countenances, and seemed quite at a loss which to embrace first. His trouble, however, was soon relieved. The stouter, and evidently the elder of the travellers, advanced and folded him in his arms.

"Surely," said he, in a hoarse, low voice, "this is my beloved Marco! No wonder you did not know me, child; for when I went away, you were but an infant, six years old. And how has it been with you? Thank heaven, I find you well and strong. But where—where is Maffeo?"

The traveller looked eagerly around; and then the younger boy resolved his anxiety by leaping into his arms.

The two boys were clasped close at last to their father's breast. He kissed them on both cheeks, and patted their heads, and lifted their chins with his finger, the better to scan their faces. Then the tears coursed down his bronzed face; and raising his hands aloft, he made a silent prayer of thanksgiving, that he had returned home from far-distant lands, and an absence of many years, to find his darling sons alive and well.

Meanwhile the other traveller found a welcome not less loving. A comely dame had thrown her arms around his neck and was holding him tight, overjoyed to find her husband by her side once more; and, two fair young girls, his daughters, were disputing with their mother his caresses. Then it came the turn of the other relatives and old friends of the wanderers to greet them and overwhelm them with endearments; and, before these greetings were over, night had fallen, and the court-yard was lit up by the torches which the servants had fetched and lighted. The scene then changed to the great hall, which, while the merry-making had been going on in the court-yard, had been quickly transformed into a banqueting-room. Two long rows of tables decked out with a profusion of flowers, and profusely laden with a bounteous, smoking hot supper, were ranged throughout its length; while the apartment was lit up by hundreds of wax candles, which gleamed from gilded candelabra fixed along the walls. The servants, clad in the livery of the house, stood beside the tables, ready to serve the many guests; who poured in and took their places, and waited till the two travellers reappeared.

The latter had gone up to their chambers, to enjoy a moment with their families in private, and to exchange their outlandish garments for their native costume. They ere long descended, clad in splendid suits of velvet, and took their places at the heads of the two tables, their children on either side of them. Very late that night, it may well be believed, was the revel of welcome kept up. The travellers, at last finding themselves cozily at home, with all who were dear around them, their appetites sated with delicious dishes and warming wines, their bodies rested from the long journey, grew very merry and talkative, and launched out into long stories of their adventures.

For nine long years they had been absent from Venice, and only once or twice had they either heard news from home, or been able to send tidings of themselves to their families and friends. The elder, Nicolo, had left his two boys scarcely more than infants, in the care of their aunt and of their uncle Marco, the cavalier who has been described as awaiting, in the great hall, the travellers' return.

The two brothers had set out, at first, with the intention of making a trading journey to Constantinople, and then to the countries bordering on the Black Sea; for they were not only Venetian nobles, but merchants as well. It was no uncommon thing in those days for Venetian noblemen to engage in commerce; and in this way the nobility of that city long maintained themselves in wealth and power, when the nobles of other Italian cities fell into poverty and decay.

Nicolo had taken his wife with him to Constantinople and soon after their arrival there, she had died. The two little boys who had been left at home, thus became motherless. At first Nicolo was overcome with grief. He lost all desire, for the time, to return home; and now resolved to extend his travels further East than he had originally planned. After remaining awhile at Constantinople, the brothers crossed the Black Sea and tarried sometime in the Crimea, the promontory which was, centuries after, to become a famous battle ground between the Russians on one side, and the English, French, and Turks on the other. While in the Crimea, they succeeded in making some profitable trading ventures; and they learned, moreover, that further East there were countries rich in goods and treasures, though warlike in temper and barbarous in customs. Nicolo finally persuaded his brother Maffeo to venture further, and to join him in penetrating the remote countries of which they heard so much.

They first ascended the great river Volga, which flows for so long a distance through the vast territory now comprised in the Russian Empire, and entered what is now called, on the maps, Central Asia. They stopped at Bokhara, then the seat of a rude and warlike court, but where they were well treated; then sped on their way still further east, and continued their journey, pausing at the various Asiatic capitals, crossing now vast deserts, now bleak and lofty steppes, now lovely and luxuriant valleys, now dense and seemingly interminable forests, until they found themselves among the curious, squint-eyed, pig-tailed, small-footed, ingenious race whom we how call the Chinese.

Of course their journey was far from rapid. They proceeded for the most part on horseback, although sometimes they perched themselves on the humps of camels, or rode aloft on the broad backs of elephants. It took not only months, but years, to reach the limit of their journey. They were often delayed by savage Asiatic wars, which made further progress dangerous. Sometimes they were forcibly detained in the rude towns by the ruling khans, who insisted on being entertained with accounts of European marvels. Now and then they were in terrible peril of their lives from the attacks of barbarian brigands, who assailed them in lonely solitudes. Meanwhile, they were able to observe the great riches which many of the Asiatic potentates displayed; the beautiful fabrics which Asiatic skill and taste and love of gorgeous colors could produce; the astonishing variety and luxuriance of the Oriental vegetation, and the many strange animals, birds and reptiles which peopled the forests, and had their lairs and nests in the deep, rank, overgrown jungles.

Europeans had long suspected the existence, in a remote part of Asia, of a powerful and splendid empire, which they had come to speak of as Cathay. Indeed, accounts kept coming from time to time of the exploits of the sovereign of Cathay, and no less of the wisdom and energy of his rule. It was towards this mysterious land that the brothers now wended their way; resolved to discover, if possible, whether such a land really existed, and to see for themselves the mighty monarch who reigned over it.

After long years of wandering, they at last reached Cathay, which they found to really and truly exist; nor, as they saw, had any of the accounts of it which had come to their ears in Venice, at all exaggerated its extent, wealth, and power. The monarch, they saw, was indeed a great and wise ruler, a man of far higher intelligence than the Asiatic princes they had before met, and a host who welcomed them with gracious hospitality, and made them quite at home at his court.

His name was Kublai Khan, and his sway extended over a large portion of Eastern China. He was delighted with his Venetian guests, and plied them with questions about the continent from whence they came. They found, too, that he was deeply interested in Christianity, about which he eagerly and constantly asked them; declaring that he himself would introduce Christianity into Cathay.

After the brothers had spent a long period at the court of Kublai Khan, they began to feel homesick, and to wish to bear back to Venice the story of the wonderful things they had seen and heard. At first, Kublai Khan was very loth to part with them. He was very fond of their society and conversation, and he had learned a great many things from them, useful to his government. Seeing, however, that they were bent on returning home, he finally consented to take leave of them; but before he did so, he made them solemnly promise that they would come back to Cathay again. This they did, although at that time they were very doubtful whether they would fulfil their pledge.

The khan then gave them an important mission to the pope of Rome. He desired very much, he said, that the pope should send a large number of educated missionaries to Cathay, to convert his people to Christianity, and to civilize and polish his semi-barbarous subjects, so that they might become like Europeans.

The brothers were only too glad to bear this message to the pope; for they were both good Christians, and they knew with what pleasure the head of the Church would receive the news that the monarch of Cathay was not only willing, but eager, that his people should embrace the Christian faith.

Their journey back home was unattended by any serious accident, though it was a long, weary, and dangerous one. At last, in the spring of 1269 their eyes were rejoiced to greet the waters of the Mediterranean at Acre, where they remained several months, and from whence they sailed, in a Venetian galley, directly to their native city. They soon safely reached the familiar bay, and were welcomed with open arms, as we have seen, by their long-waiting relatives and friends.

CHAPTER II.

MARCO POLO'S YOUTH

arco Polo—for the reader has already guessed that the elder of the two boys who had welcomed their father home was Marco Polo—was born amid surroundings of wealth and luxury. His family was a noble one, and held high rank in Venice. His father, Nicolo, before he made his memorable journey to the court of Kublai Khan, had both inherited and amassed riches. Marco suffered in early life none of those privations which have hardened so many great travellers and discoverers, and have accustomed them to lives of peril and rough adventure. From his most tender years, he had not known what it was to wish for anything beyond his reach. Fine clothes, plenty of playmates, petting, fond parents, all the pleasures enjoyed by the children of his time, were his.

Instead of going to school, he was taught at home by tutors and governesses; and happily his own tastes led him to find study interesting, so that he became a better scholar than most boys of his age. He especially loved history and narratives of adventure and discovery, and it was often difficult to persuade him to leave his books and go to bed. He was fond, too, of geography, and was wont to puzzle for hours over such rude maps and charts as he could lay his hands on; though at that period, the maps and charts in existence were but few, and represented but here and there patches of the world.

The Polo family lived all together in the great mansion that has been described. Marco's uncle, whose name also was Marco, was the eldest brother, and when Nicolo and Maffeo went on their travels, remained in Venice to retain charge of the important trading-house which they carried on in common. This elder Marco was a kindly, though rather proud and stately man; and while he treated his little nephews, deprived as they were both of father and mother, with gentleness, he kept a close watch upon their habits and conduct. As the phrase is, he "brought them up well;" and once in a great while, when young Marco's high spirits betrayed him into wild pranks, his uncle would shut him up in one of the remote rooms of the house. On this occasion the little fellow would beg, as a special favor, that one of his books might keep him company, and when his uncle refused this, the punishment he inflicted was indeed a severe one.

Besides their uncle, Marco and young Maffeo were left in the care of their aunt, the wife of that uncle who had gone away with their father; and their daily companions were their two cousins, the daughters of this aunt, not far from their own age. But their aunt was a fine lady of the doge's court, and was always going to balls, the theatre, or galas in the lagoon; and so they saw but little of her. Marco and his brother spent many happy hours in their gondolas, which they themselves learned to manage with skill; and once in a while as they grew older, their uncle took them with him on hunting expeditions on the main land.

At this period, ferocious wars were continually going on between Venice and its great maritime rival, the republic of Genoa. Both struggled for the supremacy of Mediterranean commerce, and sought to gain as many military stations and fortresses as possible on the islands and seaboards of the Levant. In these wars, Venice up to this time had been generally successful; the time was, indeed, drawing near when the Genoese would become the conquerors; but it had not yet come.

It was one of Marco's chief delights to watch the brilliant arrays of troops as they were reviewed by the doge in the Piazza before leaving for the seat of conflict: and to haunt the quays and watch the preparations for departure of the quaint war-galleys of the age. He caught the martial spirit which was then in the air, and often longed to be old enough to go to the wars and fight under the proud flag of Venice; and thus came to have adventurous and military tastes. He was not destined to indulge these tastes for many years to come; but the time was, long after, to arrive, when he would engage in furious battle with his country's foes, and have a romantic and thrilling experience in the fortunes of war.

At the period of his father's return from Cathay, Marco, as has been said, was fifteen years of age, a bright, promising boy, intelligent beyond his age, and a great favorite with all who knew him. It may well be believed that he was delighted to see his father once more, after the lapse of so many years; and to hear from his lips the tale of his many and marvellous adventures in the East. Nicolo, on his side, was rejoiced to find his elder son grown up to be so vigorous and attractive a youth, and was extremely proud of him. He freely indulged Marco's desire to hear him recount his adventures; and used to sit talking with him for hours together. He soon perceived that Marco had a keen taste for a life of stirring adventure, and was far from displeased to make the discovery.

One day, when Nicolo had been at home for several months, he was chatting with Marco, and happened to say that he had given his promise to Kublai Khan to return to Cathay.

"And you will go, sir, will you not?" eagerly asked Marco. "You will keep your promise to the great king?"

"In truth, I know not," was the father's reply. "There are many things to keep me at home. These wars interfere much with our trade, and it needs all three of us brothers to be here to look after it. The journey to Cathay, too, is not only long and dreary, but dangerous. The man who goes thither, holds his life, every hour, in his hand. At any moment, a hidden enemy may despatch him before he can lift a weapon; or, he may be lost on the great deserts, and die of sheer thirst and starvation. Then, my son, how can I leave you and your brother again, for so long a time? It would be too hard to part from you; to be far away, and not able to watch you, as month by month you grow towards manhood. On the other hand, there are vast riches to be had in Cathay; and noble service to be done for our Holy Church, by once more venturing thither."

"But, father," replied Marco, grasping Nicolo's arm, "you need not leave me behind. I beg you to go, and to let me go with you! Surely I am old enough and big enough now to go anywhere. Think, sir, I shall be soon sixteen: why, that is almost a man. Look, I am almost as tall as you are now. I can handle a sword, javelin, and cross-bow as well as any boy of my age; I am strong and well, and can walk and ride with the stoutest. My uncle Maffeo said, the other day, I would make a fine soldier, young as I am. Pray, sir, let me go with you to Cathay!"

Nicolo smiled, and patted the eager boy's flushed cheek; but gently shook his head.

"You ask, dear Marco," said he, "what cannot be. What! Do you suppose I would risk your young life amid those fierce Tartar tribes, those frightful jungles, those dreary, trackless wastes? And even if you reached Cathay in safety, do you think I would trust you with that Eastern despot, Kublai Khan, who might take it into his wilful head to separate you from me, and keep you forever? No, no, Marco, I should not dare take you, even if I went."

Marco hung his head in deep disappointment. He had long had it in his heart to implore his father to let him return with him to Cathay; and now Nicolo's words chilled and grieved him. But he was not easily discouraged. In spite of his father's refusal, he resolved to leave no persuasion untried. Again and again he returned to the subject that absorbed his mind; but all his pleading might have been in vain, had it not been that a powerful ally took up his cause. This was his uncle Maffeo: who, besides admiring Marco greatly, said that the companionship of a brave and vigorous youth would be of great value to his brother and himself, in case they again crossed Asia, and that Marco might win the special friendship of Kublai Khan by his youth, lively spirits, and agreeable bearing.

In due time, the two brothers definitely made up their minds to fulfil their promise to the oriental monarch; and after many long and earnest talks, Nicolo filled his son's heart with joy by telling him that he might go with them.

Much remained to be done, however, before they set out. On arriving at Acre, returning from their first journey, the brothers Polo had borne in mind the message of Kublai Khan to the pope; and the first thing they did was to visit a famous Church dignitary who was staying there, named Tedaldo, archdeacon of Liege This eminent man had no sooner heard their errand, than he astonished them very much by telling them that, just now, there was no pope at all, and that consequently, they could not deliver their message! Not long before their arrival, Pope Clement IV had died; and the cardinals had not yet been able to agree upon a successor. This vacancy in the papal chair was not, indeed, yet filled. The Polos, after having resolved to go again to Cathay, delayed their departure until a new pope should be chosen, so that he might send some missionaries with them, as Kublai Khan desired.

But they grew tired of waiting; for, after two years, the great council of the Church seemed no nearer electing a pope than at first; and the Polos made up their minds that they must return to Cathay, if at all, without the missionaries. Then the naval wars going on between Venice and Genoa made it for a while unsafe for Venetians to cross the Mediterranean to Syria, and this compelled another postponement of their plans. At last, however, a favorable opportunity occurred to traverse the sea to Acre, which as before was to be the starting-point of the travellers. A war-galley destined for that Asiatic town, then in the possession of Venice, was about to set forth; and by Nicolo's great influence at court, where he had been heartily welcomed back by the reigning doge, a passage was secured in her for all three.

Marco had scarcely slept since permission to go had been wrung from his reluctant father. He devoted himself ardently to the practise of the sword and the cross-bow; he was measured for two suits of clothes, fit for rough travelling; again and again he went over the proposed route, on such charts relating to it as his father had brought with him: and he constantly talked about the wonderful things he was about to see, and the many adventures he would undoubtedly meet with. Happily his younger brother, Maffeo, whose tastes were gentle and domestic, did not share his eagerness for a wandering life; and, well content to stay at home, was only distressed at the thought of the long absence of his father and of the brother who had been his constant companion.

On the eve of the day appointed for the departure of the travellers, the great house on the canal of San Giovanni

MARCO STUDYING THE CHARTS.

Crisostomo was once more crowded with a numerous and brilliantly attired assemblage. Nicolo had resolved to give a bounteous parting feast to his family and friends; and the doge himself had consented to honor the feast with his presence. There was no family more honored and respected in Venice than the Polos; and the doge regarded Nicolo as one of the bravest and most estimable of his subjects.

The appearance of the guests was very different from that on the former occasion. The joyful welcome was replaced by the sad leave-taking. Little Maffeo's face was suffused with tears, which he in vain tried to repress; and the elder Marco looked grave and downcast. As for young Marco, his anticipations of the journey so excited him that he could scarcely think of grief, even at leaving his home and parting from his brother and kind kindred. His fair face was flushed with eager expectation: and he felt very proud of the brand-new sword which swung, for the first time, at his side. He felt himself already a man and a soldier, and never once thought of shrinking from the dangers of the tour. To him it was more like a holiday journey than a dangerous venture; and it seemed as if the morrow would never come.

At last the guests tearfully embraced the brothers and Marco, and one by one departed. The candles in the glittering candelabra were put out, and the house was left in darkness.

The sun had scarcely risen when Marco leaped from his bed, donned the suit which had been prepared for his setting out, and buckled on his sword; and while almost all the people of Venice were still wrapped in slumber, the travellers wended their way to the war-galley on the quay, and went on board.

CHAPTER III.

MARCO POLO SETS FORTH

As Marco Polo stood, on that bright April morning in 1271, on the deck of the war-galley, and watched the glittering domes and spires of Venice receding from view, while the vessel sailed down the Adriatic, he little guessed how many years would elapse ere his eyes would greet the familiar home scenes again.

But he thought only of the future just before him; and although, on passing out of the Gulf of Venice into the rougher waters of the Adriatic, he was at first a little sea-sick, he soon recovered his buoyancy of spirits, and now gazed with keen interest at the objects which coast and waters presented.

It was a delightful trip, through the Adriatic, across the sparkling purple waves of the Mediterranean, skirting the rugged coast of Greece, and at last launching into the more open ocean, out of sight of land; and the days that elapsed between the departure from Venice and the arrival at the curious old town of Acre, on the Syrian coast, with its towered walls, its narrow, winding streets, its lofty castle, its temples, palaces and churches, quite unlike those of Venice, were joyous ones to the young traveller.

On landing at Acre, the brothers Polo and Marco repaired to the best inn in the place; and Nicolo lost no time in seeking out his old friend, the priest Tedaldo, to learn what prospect there was of missionaries going eastward with them. Tedaldo was rejoiced to see him, but said that no pope had yet been chosen; and begged Nicolo to stay at Acre until that event took place. At first Nicolo, impatient to reach the great khan's court, resisted Tedaldo's request; but finally the shrewd priest prevailed with him.

"If you will give us leave to go Jerusalem, and get some holy oil from the lamp on the Sepulchre," said Nicolo, "we will not proceed on our journey until you consent. The great khan will receive the holy oil as a precious gift."

"Be it so," responded Tedaldo; "go to Jerusalem, and after performing your errand, return hither. Perhaps, then, we shall have a pope."

Marco was well pleased to visit the holy city, which he now did, in company with his father. They did not stay long at Jerusalem; but while there, Marco had time to see all the ancient and sacred relics and curious sights which still attract the traveller. Having procured a vial of oil from the lamp on the Sepulchre (which, it was said, had been kept constantly burning there from the time of Christ's death), Nicolo returned to Acre. No pope had yet been chosen; and now Tedaldo could not find it in his heart to forbid the departure of the brothers.

They therefore set out from Acre, crossing in a galley to the old fortified town of Ayas, in the gulf of Scanderoon. Ayas they found to be a busy commercial port, with teeming bazaars and a noble fortress rising near the shore; but they could not tarry long there, and began to make their preparations to penetrate into Armenia. They were on the point of starting, when an urgent message reached them from Acre.

It seemed that a pope had at last been elected, and that the choice had fallen on no other than their friend Tedaldo himself, who took the name of Gregory the Tenth; and he had sent for them to return at once to Acre, and receive his instructions how to deal with the great khan.

On reaching Acre, the Polos were at once admitted to the presence of their old friend, who had now become the head of the Church. Tedaldo, or Pope Gregory, as he should now be called, received them with all his old kindness of manner, in the palace where he was sojourning, and gave his special blessing to young Marco, whose youth and bearing greatly pleased him.

Then, turning to the two brothers, the pope said:

"Now I can give you full power and authority to be the envoys of the Church to Kublai Khan. You shall take with you two trusty friars, who will aid you in converting the heathen of Cathay; and you yourselves may ordain bishops and priests, and grant absolution. To show my desire to receive Kublai into the bosom of the Church, I will give you some vases and jars of crystal, to take to him as presents from me."

Nicolo fell at the pope's feet, and did him humble and grateful reverence and Maffeo and Marco followed his example. All their wishes seemed now fulfilled; and, after

bidding the pope once more adieu, and receiving his blessing, they set out to return to Ayas, inspired by the new and
noble purpose of converting a vast nation of barbarians
to the true faith. With them went the two friars whom
the pope had appointed, Nicolo of Vicenza, and William
of Tripoli; and on landing at Ayas, they resolved to delay
their journey no longer.

Another mishap, however, was destined to befall them
before they found themselves full on their way eastward.
At Ayas they learned that Armenia, the country through
which they were about to pass, had just been invaded by
the Sultan of Babylon with a formidable army.

No sooner had the two friars heard this unwelcome
news than they ran to Nicolo, and declared that they were
afraid to go on, or even to stay at Ayas. In vain Nicolo besought them to continue with him, and even to brave the
dangers that now loomed before them, rather than give up
the project of converting the people of Cathay.

"No," replied the friars: "We are afraid of these ruthless
Saracens. If they should capture any Christian priests, it
would be to torture and kill them. Take our credentials
and documents, Messer Polo; and God be with you. We
must return to Acre."

And so they did, taking the first galley that set out for
that place.

The Polos found that they must go forward alone; and
after a last look at Ayas, and feeling, truth to tell, somewhat
alarmed lest they should meet the Saracen invaders, they
started on the high road that led northward in the direc-

tion of Turcomania.

Marco observed everything on the journey with the keenest curiosity; and his father, who had already traversed that region, was able to explain many sights that were mysterious to him. They passed through many queer Asiatic cities and towns, and Marco stared at the dusky complexions and picturesque attire of the natives. The natives, in turn, examined the travellers with much amazement; but everywhere, in this part of the country, seemed friendly, and not at all disposed to molest them.

Sometimes the wayfarers would stop in a city or town a week or two at a time, lodging in very old inns, and partaking of dishes which Marco had never seen before, and of some of which neither of the three knew the names.

The people of the regions through which they passed were usually poverty stricken, and seemed quite content with very little. Marco observed that they were a very lazy set, and spent a great deal of time drinking a coarse, rank liquor, which speedily intoxicated them.

Sometimes, however, the travellers came to a town which had a well-to-do, thriving aspect, and where they met men and women of a higher and more active class. The chiefs in these places would treat them with hearty hospitality, placing before them the best dishes and most luscious fruits the region afforded, and giving them the best rooms in their houses—not very comfortable ones, at best—in which to sleep.

One day, a hospitable chief proposed to the Polos that they should form part of a hunting expedition, which was

Marco Shooting in the Asiatic Hills

about to set out in search of savage game on the neighboring hills. This proposal gave young Marco a thrill of pleasure, for he had begun to think that their journey was getting monotonous. At first his father refused to let him go with the hunting party; but Marco begged so persistently, and the chief brought out a horse for his use that seemed so strong and steady, that Nicolo finally yielded.

Not only horses, but elephants also, bore the sportsmen to their scene of action; and after travelling for two days across the plains and among the hills, the party encamped on a river bank. Then Marco, for the first time, saw the fierce, wild sport which the Asiatic hills and jungles provided. He was too young and too little skilled to take any active part in the hunt for wild beasts; but roamed the lofty forests, and brought down many a bird of gorgeous plumage, which proved afterwards to afford the sweetest and most delicate nourishment. Once he witnessed, from a safe distance, a terrific encounter with a gigantic tiger, which the natives attacked from the backs of their elephants, and at last succeeded in killing and dragging, with his magnificent striped hide, into the camp.

Marco was afterwards to become quite accustomed to this thrilling sport, and to deal, with his own hand, many a finishing blow upon lion and tiger and famished wolf.

After crossing the eastern edge of Turcomania, the travellers entered the picturesque and fruitful country of Greater Armenia with its broad, fertile plains, and its grim and narrow mountain passes; the same country, indeed, which in our own times has been so often the scene of conflict between the Russians and the Turks. They passed near or by the very spots where the now famous fortresses of Kars and Erzeroum stand; and as they proceeded, they were surprised to find the region so thickly dotted with towns and villages, and sometimes quite stately cities. They found the inhabitants, who were for the most part Tartars, as little disposed to molest them as the Turcomans had been; though, now and then, as they went through lonely districts, they were menaced by brigands.

With them were several native guides, whose language was already familiar to the two elder Polos. One day, one of these guides stopped, and pointed to a mountain, whose dim outline could just be made out in the hazy distance.

"Do you see that mountain?" he said, turning to the travellers. "It is Mount Ararat. It was there that Noah's ark was stranded, after the flood. The ark is still there, on the top of the mountain; and the faithful of this region brave the snows with which Ararat is perpetually shrouded, to get from the ark some of its pitch, which they make into amulets, and wear as a charm around their necks!"

Marco listened with open mouth, and stared long and earnestly at the famous eminence. He could scarcely believe that the ark was still there; yet the guide spoke so earnestly that he was loth to doubt what he said.

After crossing a lofty range of mountains, they descended into a wide and umbrageous valley, through which meandered a broad, rapidly flowing river. This river, Marco learned, was no other than the Tigris, which flows northward from the Persian Gulf. On every hand the young traveller perceived the majestic ruins of the splendid civilization which had once existed in this valley.

Ruined or decaying cities, with vast walls, and lofty palaces, and towering temples, were often encountered; and near them nestled the more modern towns and villages, still alive with the bustle of trade or the vanity of oriental show. This country was the kingdom of Mosul; and in some of the towns, Marco observed manufactories of fine cloth, which was produced with rapidity and skill, and was made of many beautiful colors. This cloth gave the name to what we now call "muslin," from the place whence it was first obtained; it was really not muslin, but a much finer texture, of silk and gold. The Polos were delighted to find that large numbers of the people of Mosul were Christians, who gave them a welcome all the warmer because of their professing the same faith.

As they descended the valley of the Tigris further towards the Persian Gulf, however, they were destined to meet with a very different kind of people. From the mountain fastnesses of Curdistan there swooped into the valley fierce bands of Curds, the savage and vindictive race who dwelt in those fastnesses, and whose occupation it was to rob and murder. Their very name, which, in Turkish, means "wolves," betrayed their character and habits. Luckily a large number of Mosul Christians accompanied the travellers, armed to the teeth, purposely to protect them from the inhuman Curds; and the latter, whenever they assailed the party, were driven back, with great loss of life, to their mountain retreats again. Marco thought he had never seen such ferocious looking creatures as were some of the Curds who were taken prisoners. They were very dark, wore long, fierce moustaches, and their black eyes gleamed with a savage and murderous glare.

This danger was therefore escaped; and, soon after, Marco went nearly wild with joy to enter, and see with his own eyes, the famous city of Bagdad. He had often heard of Bagdad, from the Venetian merchants who had made journeys hither; and often, at home, had his curiosity been aroused to see the singular sights, the curious people, the ancient temples, gates and palaces, which had been thus described to him. And here he was, in the streets of the old Arab city, still in all the glory of its trade, though many of its ancient splendors had departed; and everything he saw filled him with delight. He was delighted when his father and uncle, putting up at the best inn the old city afforded, announced their intention to rest some time in Bagdad; for now he would have leisure to explore it thoroughly, and to hunt up the very scenes of the marvellous tales.

He found Bagdad to be not only full of ancient monuments, but a very thriving and busy place, ruled over by a caliph, who had a large and valiant army. It produced a bewildering variety of cloths, such as silk, gold cloth, and brocade, and it was a fine sight to see the men and women of the higher classes, arrayed in these splendid tissues, as they strolled on the river bank, or lolled in their luxurious balconies, that overlooked the Tigris. It was while in this famous place that Marco heard a story which gave him an insight into Oriental character. About forty years before there had been reigning at Bagdad, a caliph who was very avaricious, and also very rich. He had a lofty tower, which was said to be piled full of gold and silver. A Tartar prince came with a great army, attacked Bagdad and took it, and made the caliph a prisoner. When he saw the tower full of treasure, the Tartar conqueror was amazed; and ordering the captive caliph into his presence, said, "Caliph, why hast thou gathered here so many riches? When thou knewest I was coming to attack thee, why didst thou not use it to pay soldiers to defend thee?" The caliph not replying, the Tartar went on, "Now, caliph, since thou hast so vast a love for this treasure, thou must eat it!" He caused the caliph to be shut up in the tower, and commanded that neither food nor drink should be given him; for, he said, he must eat the gold, or nothing. The poor caliph died in the tower some days after, of starvation, though surrounded by heaps of treasure, that would have bought food for a mighty army.

Marco had by this time picked up enough of the language of the region to converse with the natives: and nothing pleased him more than to wander about the bazaars and shops, and to find some talkative Mussulman, who would sit and tell him stories. In this way, he heard many tales which were scarcely less romantic than those of the Arabian Nights.

One of the stories that seemed most wonderful to him was that of the "one-eyed cobbler." Some years before, it was related, there reigned at Bagdad a caliph who bore bitter hatred against the Christians, and who was resolved to put them to the sword. Thinking to entrap them by their own doctrine, he called a vast number of Christians together, and pointed to the passage in the Bible which says, that if a Christian has faith as a grain of mustard seed, and should command a mountain to be moved, it would obey the command.

"Now," said the caliph, "you who have such faith, must either move that mountain, which you see yonder—"pointing to a very lofty eminence, "or you shall one and all perish by the sword. Unless you do this in ten days, or become Mohammedans, every one of you shall die."

The Christians were terrified and bewildered at the caliph's words, and knew not what to do. For several days they felt like men already lost. But one day a certain bishop came to them, and said that he had had a vision from God; and that God had told him that if the Christians would persuade a certain pious cobbler, who had but one eye, to pray that the mountain should be moved, the prayer would be granted.

The cobbler was eagerly sought out. At first he refused to pray for the miracle, saying that he was no better than the rest. But finally he consented to offer up the prayer. The caliph's army and the Christians assembled on a vast plain before the mountain. The cobbler knelt and made a solemn appeal to heaven: when lo, the mountain rising up, moved to the spot that the caliph had pointed out! It was said that after this miracle, the caliph became secretly a Christian; and that when he died a small ivory cross was found hung around his neck.

Marco was very loth to leave Bagdad, with its romantic

memories, its venerable buildings, its brilliant bazaars, and its captivating story-tellers; and when one day, Nicolo told him that they should set out again early the next morning, he felt exceedingly sorry to hear the news. Fresh scenes, however, soon diverted his mind from the old city; and ere many days he found himself with his father and uncle on a strange galley, with lateen sails, crossing the Persian Gulf.

CHAPTER IV.

Marco Polo's Travels in Persia and Turkistan

THE passage across the Persian Gulf was a brief and prosperous one; and in due time the Polo party landed on the soil of the ancient country of Persia. The port at which they set foot on shore was an old fortified town named Hormuz, with its towers rising high above the sea, and its harbor crowded with the shipping of many nations. Here for the first time Marco witnessed the dress, manners and customs of the people who, once upon a time, had been led to brilliant victory by Cyrus and Darius.

Hormuz itself, with its bazaars, its wide streets, its fortresses and palaces, was not unlike the cities Marco had seen in Armenia but the people, both in their appearance and in their customs, were very different from those of Western Asia. They lived, it appeared, mainly on dates and salt fish and it was only when they were ill that they would taste bread. For a beverage, they drank a very strong wine, made of dates and spices. The city seemed to have but few inhabitants who actually dwelt in it. The buildings, except on the outskirts, were mostly given up to store-houses, shops, and other places of business and the surrounding plain was covered with dwellings, almost every one with a pretty, shady garden, whither the mass of the population resorted at nightfall. Marco soon learned that the people lived in this way on account of the oppressive heat which existed in the city and found by his own experience that it was one of the hottest places on earth.

He learned that sometimes winds swept across the deserts, so scorching that the people were obliged to plunge themselves up to the neck in cool water, and stay there until the winds had gone down otherwise they would be burnt to death; and a story was told him of a hostile army, which was literally baked to death, while on its way to attack Hormuz.

Marco examined the Persian ships which he saw in the harbor with great curiosity. They were wretched affairs compared with the skilfully-built Venetian galleys. Instead of being made fast with pitch, they were smeared with fish oil; and were held together by a rude twine, made of the husk of a nut. The ships were deckless, the cargo being only protected by a matting and had but one mast, one sail, and one rudder. The nails were of wood and altogether, these frail craft seemed to Marco dangerous boats in which to cross the stormy seas of the East.

Setting out from Hormuz, the Polos found themselves travelling over a vast and beautiful plain, which glowed with the most brilliant flowers, among which birds of gorgeous plumage nestled and where dates and palms grew in the richest luxuriance. The plain was watered by many picturesque streams, on the banks of which the travellers gratefully rested after their long daily jaunts. The plain crossed, they began a gentle ascent to a range of lofty hills, after traversing which they found themselves at Kerman, which was then the seat of Persian sovereignty. This, too, was a busy place, where all sorts of warlike weapons were made, and where the women were very skilful in needle-work and embroidery. Marco saw a great number of beautiful light blue turquoises, which precious stones, he heard, were found in great quantities among the neighboring mountains.

The Polos only staid in Kerman long enough to take a good rest, and then set out again for already they had been nearly a year on their travels, and Nicolo was anxious to get to Cathay as soon as possible, lest the good khan who had treated him so well before, should be dead. But they had yet many a long month of journeying before them, and they were to see many strange and wonderful things before they reached the end of their travels. They now crossed a beautiful country, varied with plains, hills, and lovely valleys, where dates grew in plenty, and many other fruits, which Marco had never before seen, hung on the trees and bushes. He saw, browsing in the meadows, many large, white oxen, with short smooth hair, thick stubby horns, and humps on their backs and the sheep in the pastures were the biggest he had ever seen. Almost every village they passed was surrounded by a high wall of mud. On asking why this was, Marco was told that the country was infested with banditti, and that these walls were built to protect the people from their bold and savage incursions. A native declared to him that these banditti were magicians; and that when they wished to attack a village, they were able, by their magic spells, to turn daylight into darkness. Sometimes, this native said, there was as many as ten thousand men in these bands of robbers.

The travellers heard these stories of the banditti with some alarm, for they were about to pass through the very region where they dwelt nor was this alarm groundless. Scarcely had they got fairly away from one of the villages, when they were suddenly attacked by a formidable band, and were forced to fight desperately for their lives. The three Polos succeeded in killing a number of the robbers, and in escaping into a village just beyond but when they called their guides and attendants together, they found that the robbers had killed or captured all but seven of them and they were obliged to push forward with this small number.

They soon came to a dismal and dreary desert, which it took them a week to cross, and where they saw nowhere a vestige of human habitation. For three days they found no water whatever, except some little salt streams, from which they could not drink, however parched by thirst. It was a vast solitude, where no living thing appeared and Marco gave a sigh of relief and satisfaction when, towards the end of the seventh day, the buildings of another large and flourishing city came into view. But beyond this city, another and still larger desert stretched out before them. Profiting by their previous experience, the Polos carried with them an ample quantity of water; and passed across the greater desert without much suffering. They had now

reached the northernmost provinces of Persia. One day
Marco observed a very tall, wide spreading tree, the bark
of which was a bright green on one side, and white on
the other. This tree stood entirely alone, on a vast plain,
where there was not the least sign of any other trees, as
far as eye could reach in any direction. Marco thought this
very strange, and called his party to look at it. Then one
of the Persian guides, whom they had brought with them,
told him that it was very near this curious tree, which was
called the "Dry Tree," that a famous battle was once fought
between Alexander the Great and King Darius.

Not long after passing the "Dry Tree", the travellers
entered a district called Mulchet, not far from the Caspian
sea and here Marco, who, everywhere he went, put himself
on easy terms with the most intelligent natives he could
find, heard many interesting stories and legends about
the country through which he was travelling. One of the
most romantic of these legends was that which related
to the "Old Man of the Mountain," who it was said, dwelt
in the neighboring range not many years before. An old
nobleman—so ran the story—who had plenty of money,
had caused a certain deep valley to be enclosed with high
walls at either end, so that none could enter whom he
wished to keep out and thus protected, he cultivated a rare
and beautiful garden in the valley. In the midst of this he
reared gilded pavilions, and even lofty and glittering palaces, whose minarets could be seen a great distance away.
The old man also surrounded himself with many lovely
women, who sang and danced exquisitely, and every day

feasted, with the chosen few whom he invited to share the delights of the valley.

Thus was created what the old man called his Paradise; following, as near as he could, the description which Mohammed had given of that celestial abode. It was said that he gathered about him a number of boys and youths, to whom he told tales of Paradise; and that, sometimes, making these youths drink a certain wine, which stupefied them, he had them carried to the beautiful garden, where they awoke to find themselves in the midst of the most ravishing scenes. He thereby made them believe that it was really Paradise where they dwelt, and that he was a great Prophet and so could persuade them to do just what he pleased. When he had a grudge against any neighboring prince, he would send these youths forth to kill his enemy, promising that if they did his bidding they should forever live in this charming Paradise.

Soon he became a terror through all the land, wreaking his vengeance on all who offended him, and reducing the rulers round about to submission. But by and by the king of the Western Tartars became enraged at the tyranny and murders of the Old Man of the Mountain, and resolved to put an end to them. He accordingly sent one of his generals at the head of a numerous army, to destroy the Old Man's Paradise. In vain, however, did the Tartars assail the solid towers and walls that defended the valley; they could not penetrate it. They were obliged to lay regular siege to it and it was only after three months that the Old Man of the Mountain, his courtiers and houris, were forced, from sheer want of food, to surrender. The old man himself, and all the youths and men of his court, were at once put to death; the palaces and pavilions were razed to the earth; and the fairy-like gardens were ruthlessly turned into a desolate waste.

The Polos had gone as far northward as they intended, and now turned their faces directly towards the east. They entered a wild mountain region where there were but few human habitations, but which was broken into jagged mountain masses, in the defiles of which were the fastnesses of robbers. They were often attacked by these fierce bands, but so well armed were they and their company, and so valiant, that they escaped this frequent peril. They reached Balkh, then still a stately city, many of whose buildings were of marble, though much of it was in ruins. Here, Marco was told, Alexander the Great had married the Persian King Darius's daughter; and he gazed with deep interest on a place which was the scene of many thrilling events of which he had read in history.

From Balkh Marco and his fellow-travellers rapidly approached those lofty ranges of gigantic mountains which rise in Eastern Turkistan, and which divide Western Asia from China on one side, and Hindoostan on the other. As he gazed at these eminences, the peaks of which seemed to cleave the very clouds, Marco was deeply impressed by their rugged grandeur. He had never seen imagined mountains so high and he wondered how it could be possible for the party to cross them. Sometimes, at the end of a valley, they seemed to close in the way completely.

There seemed to be no possible exit; no declivity or pass seemed to open itself between them. Yet when the travellers reached the foot of the mountains, a narrow defile would be revealed and they would pass through in single file, leading their horses and camels, sometimes on a path so narrow and so high above the gorge by whose side it ran, that it seemed inevitable that the travellers would fall and break their necks.

All through these mountains, Marco observed that the people were fierce and wild, and lived wandering lives, subsisting on the game they secured by hunting. They were, for the most part, intemperate; and after a hunt, would resort to the nearest village and intoxicate themselves with the fiery palm wine which was everywhere made and drunk in that region. In some places, where sheep were raised on the steep hill-sides, Marco found that the shepherds lived in caves he mountains, so dug as to form dwellings, with several rooms. Sometimes these caves were very handsomely fitted up.

The next great town that the travellers reached, after leaving Balkh, was Badakshan, still famous, in our own day, as a centre of Oriental trade. It was then ruled over by a powerful king, who claimed to be a direct descendant of Alexander the Great and of King Darius. The city was situated in the midst of lofty and jagged eminences; and all around, perched on the tops of high crags, Marco espied the strong castles and fortresses which defended it from hostile attacks. Every pass was thus stoutly guarded, and Marco saw that the people were warlike in their tastes, being excellent archers and very skilful hunters. The men wore the skins of beasts; and the women always clothed themselves in an immense quantity of bombazine, wrapped in many folds around their bodies. On Marco's asking why they did this, he was told that it was because they wished to appear very fat; for this, in the eyes of the men, was regarded as a point of beauty. The women's heads were covered with hoods, while from their ears long sleeves hung to the ground, and swayed to and fro as the stout-looking damsels waddled along.

While the wanderers were staying at Badakshan (for having been made welcome by the king, they were in no great haste to depart) Marco fell extremely with a fever. For a while his life was despaired of; but the skill of the native doctors at last set him on his feet again. As soon as he was able to stir abroad, the doctors told him to go to the summit of one of the neighboring mountains and stay awhile. This he did; and the air was so pure and dry at that elevation, that he very rapidly recovered. Leaving Badakshan, where the Venetians had much enjoyed their rest and the hospitality of the monarch, they soon found themselves passing along the banks of a wide and swift river, the same that we now know as the Oxus; which, at the point that they reached it, issued from a vast lake, fed by the eternal snows of the surrounding eminences.

The river flowed in a vast and most picturesque valley between two lofty ranges; and Marco was fairly transported by the exceeding grandeur of the river. Ascending then to the plateau beyond, the travellers found themselves on a higher level than they had ever before reached, where the atmosphere was so rare that they actually found it difficult to breathe. This was no other than the famous Pamir Steppe, which extends, in a broad tableland, for many miles between Turkistan and Chinese Tartary. The views from this high altitude were imposing in the extreme. In the distance rose the snowy summits of the Himalayas; while far below the travellers lay the sunny and luxuriant valleys, creeping far under the mountain shadows, in some of which was the birth-place of that great Aryan tribe from which almost every European nation has descended.

Many were the interesting sights that Marco saw, as the party slowly wended its way over the mighty steppe. There were sheep with horns three or four feet long, out of which horns the shepherds made knives and spoons. Every little while, along the road, Marco saw piles of these horns heaped up, and learned that they were landmarks to guide the traveller on his way, when the snows of winter concealed the road from view. Marco was surprised to see no villages, or even huts, on the great steppe, and found that the shepherds, who were its only inhabitants, dwelt in mountain caves.

Descending at last from the Pamir Steppe, the party entered what was then the noble and flourishing city of Samarcand. This place was not many years after to be taken by the famous Tartar warrior, Timour Tamerlane, and to be made the seat of his splendid empire in Central Asia; and in our own day, the visitor to Samarcand is taken to a mosque where, he is told, repose Timour's remains.

Marco was greatly impressed with the wealth and splendor of the city, its imposing temples and palaces, and its bustling bazaars; but time was passing, and the travellers were forced to hurry away and continue their journey eastward. Beyond Samarcand, they proceeded through fruitful valleys and delightful scenes, across fields where the cotton plant was growing luxuriantly, by orchards and vineyards, and through villages where cloths of many kinds were being made. They came to spots where they saw the people searching, among the rocks and in the mountain sides, for rare jewels; and Marco saw the men extracting rubies, jasper, and calcedony from the hiding-places where nature had concealed them.

So travelling, they came at last to a town on the banks of a lake, called Lop. This town stood on the borders of the great Gobi Desert, which now alone separated the Polos from the western confines of China; and before entering upon the long tramp across this dreary waste, they resolved to stay at Lop a week and rest. Meanwhile, they made ample preparations for crossing the great desert. It would take them a month, they were told, to gain the other side; and they therefore packed enough provisions to last them that length of time. Happily, there was no need that they should burden themselves with water; for the desert, arid as it was, provided streams that ran from the lofty ranges near by, in sufficient abundance to supply all who crossed its wide expanse.

CHAPTER V.

MARCO POLO REACHES CATHAY

AFTER passing across the great Gobi Desert, where he endured many hardships, and once came near being lost, by being separated from his companions, Marco encountered a very different country and people from those he had before seen. Before he had met with Turcomans only; for the most part fierce, wandering tribes, given to plundering and murder, and going from place to place, without any settled home. Now he found himself among a quiet, busy, and to a large degree civilized people, the greater portion of whom seemed to be farmers, devoted to the tilling of the fruitful and abundantly yielding lands.

Instead of the tall, large-featured, heavily-bearded Turcomans, the people were short and squat, with squinted eyes, high cheek bones, hair braided in long queues behind, and a peculiar yellow complexion.

They were, indeed, Chinese. Their loose costumes, their hats turned up at the brim, their small shoes turned up at the toes, their taste in dress, marked them as a quite distinct race from the inhabitants of the mountain regions Marco had not long before traversed. Instead of the plain mosques, too, with their glaring white exteriors, their bare interiors, and their big bulb-like domes. Marco now saw gorgeous temples, decked out both inside and out with the greatest profusion of ornament, and containing huge idols that fairly glittered with gilding and gems. The towns, instead of consisting of low, plain buildings, were full of variety and adornment in their architecture, and displayed the high degree to which the arts had even then been carried by the Chinese.

Everywhere the fields were aglow with rich and plentiful crops. Marco could not but perceive the air of home-like contentment that everywhere prevailed, in contrast with the restless and savage customs of the Turcomans and as he passed through the Chinese villages towards evening, he was visibly reminded of home when he saw the Chinese families cozily seated in front of their doors, or in the little shaded balconies over them, enjoying, after the day's labor, the serenity and repose of the twilight hours, very much as the Venetians were wont to do.

He was much struck by the great number of temples and of monasteries which he saw as the party penetrated the country. Instead of the worship of Mohammed the Prophet, the people were Buddhists, and paid their devotion to the countless idols everywhere set up. Marco soon learned a great deal about the manners and habits of this race, which greatly excited his curiosity. Every Chinese who had children was wont, at a certain festival, to take them, with a sheep, to one of the temples, where the sheep was cooked and offered as a sacrifice to the chief idol. After the meat had been left for some time at the feet of the idol, it was taken away, and the man invited his friends together to feast upon it. The bones were then collected, and kept in the house with much reverence and care. When a man or woman died the body was burned. It was first carried to a sort of pavilion, erected for the purpose, and placed in it; and then the friends brought wine and food, and put it before the corpse. Arriving at the funeral pyre, the mourners cut out of paper a number of little figures, representing men, horses, camels and lions, which they threw upon the flames as they enveloped the dead person; believing that by so doing they insured their relation the possession of the realities thus represented, in the other world.

One day, the Venetians arrived at a city called Kamul, which struck Marco as a very gay and lively place. The people here seemed to think of nothing but having a perpetual good time. Their main occupation was that of farming; but they seemed to work very little, while their store-houses were full to overflowing, and they evidently had an abundance of good things. From morning till night, while Marco staid at Kamul, he heard nothing but sounds of music, singing, and dancing. He was awakened by the playing of strange loud musical instruments, and went to sleep with their sounds still ringing in his ears. The people were exceedingly hospitable, and vied with each other to receive the strangers as their guests. The master of the house where Marco lodged, having seen to it that he was comfortably ensconced, went off to another house, leaving Marco to do as he pleased, and for the time master. Marco could not fail to observe that the women of Kamul were not only full of gayety and fond of amusement, but were singularly handsome. Every evening there were dancing and singing in the open spaces in front of the houses, in which all seemed to join with the heartiest gusto.

Marco found that sorcerers and magicians were held in awe and high respect here, as in other countries through which he had passed. The Chinese sorcerers were very different looking personages, however, from those he had so often seen in Turkistan. They wore long moustaches, that flowed down on their breasts; but no beards on their chins. Instead of long black gowns, they appeared in tunics, blazoned all over with the figures of dragons, dolphins and other fabulous animals. They carried long wands, often of silver or gold; and on their heads they wore high caps, richly fringed. Whenever a sorcerer passed along the street, the people uncovered until he had gone by. These mysterious men lived apart from the rest of the world, often in monasteries that stood on hills on the outskirts of the town; and it was the custom of the people, whenever any special event occurred in their towns, such as a birth, a death, a journey or a fire, to seek in all haste their magicians to learn its significance and bearing upon their lives.

The sorcerers, of course, charged a large round sum for their prophecies; and so were all rich, and lived in much grandeur and luxury. As soon as any one died, the sorcerer was applied to, and informed of the exact date of the dead person's death. He then went into his room and performed a number of strange incantations; after which he was able to tell the relatives what day and hour it would be lucky to bury the dead. He would also inform them by what door the corpse should be carried out of the house; and sometimes told them that it must be brought into the street through a hole made in the wall, so as to give good fortune to the living relatives. ⁓

Not far from Kamul, Marco and his party came to a large mining district, where he had an opportunity to witness another instance of the skill and intelligence of the Chinese. There were mines of copper and antimony and also mines from which a very peculiar mineral, called asbestos, was taken. The ore of this asbestos, it seems, was taken from the mountains and broken up, and then became a sort of stringy mass. It was dried and crushed in a mortar, and then formed a rough, strong thread. This thread was woven into cloth, and being bleached by fire, became as white as snow, and very strong. The idea of making a cloth out of a mineral, dug from mountain gorges, was a new and surprising one to our young traveller.

As Marco advanced through the country, which was that of Tangat, he observed that the temples became larger and more magnificent, and that the idols in them also increased in size and splendor of decoration. He saw, at one of the more populous cities, idols ten or twelve feet high, of wood, stone, and clay, completely covered with thick plates of gold and ivory. In some of these temples, the priests, un-like those of other parts of China, lived with great sobriety and even self-denial. During one month in the year these priests would not kill any animal, or even insect, however small, and in this month they only partook of flesh, and that of the plainest kind, once in five days. The people of this region, on the other hand, lived in a very gross and beastly way, giving themselves up to self-indulgence and indolence. The richer men had many wives, whom they divorced as soon as they got sick of them; and often married their cousins and other near relatives. They devoted a great deal of time to eating, drinking and sleeping, and impressed Marco as a much lower order of beings than the other Chinese he had seen.

The travellers were about to resume their journey westward, when they heard news that greatly disappointed them, and caused them to delay their departure from Campicion, the chief town of Tangat. This news was, that a great war had broken out between two nations whose territories were directly in their path to Cathay. Their way, indeed, lay through the very region where the war had already begun to rage. To attempt to reach Cathay by any other road was impossible; for the countries north and south were unknown to their guides, and they would probably get lost, or fall into the hands of hostile races, if they tried an unknown, roundabout road.

They were, therefore, forced to content themselves with awaiting the return of peace at Campicion, an idea which was far from pleasant to Marco, who did not think it an attractive place, and was, moreover, very impatient to reach his journey's end. He made the best of circumstances, however, and finding that the war was likely to last some time, resolved to spend the time of waiting in making explorations in the neighboring regions. He accordingly set out with a small company, and made his way from place to place as best he could, narrowly observing all the curious peoples and customs that he encountered.

He soon found himself once more on the edge of the great desert, and came to a large and ancient city called Ezina, which was more than half in ruins. He soon learned that it had once been a thriving capital, and had been taken by the famous Tartar warrior, Genghis Khan. Now it was inhabited by a roving and sport-loving population, who only lived in it in summer, descending into the valleys and there dwelling in the winter season. These people were much given to the rearing of camels and horses, and were exceedingly fond of hunting in the vast pine forests that spread over the neighboring hills.

From Ezina Marco went to a still larger city of Karakorum, which seemed to him at least three miles in circumference, and which, as he heard, had once been the capital of the Tartar conquerors of China. It stood on a very picturesque spot. A beautiful river flowed near its walls, on the banks of which were numberless tents, occupied by wandering Tartar tribes who preferred this mode of life to dwelling in the city itself. The mountains were not far off; and on many a crag and spur Marco could espy the lordly castles where once had dwelt the proud Tartar nobles. ←

It was at Karakorum that Marco for the first time heard the wonderful story of the conquests of Genghis Khan, the mighty Tartar chief whose descendant, Kublai Khan, was then reigning in Cathay. He listened with wrapt attention to the accounts which some of the natives, whose acquain-

tance he made, gave of the terrific battle in which Genghis
Khan had overthrown the haughty tyrant, Prester John,
and had himself won sway over all the surrounding region.
Genghis Khan, it seemed, had asked Prester John to give
him his daughter to wife; and Prester John had returned
a haughty refusal. "What is this Genghis Khan," Prester
John had exclaimed, "but my dog and slave! Go and let
him know that I would burn my daughter to ashes before
I would give her to him. Tell him he is a dog and a traitor!"
Genghis Khan was beside himself with rage when he heard
this insulting message, and swore that he would humble
Prester John's pride in the dust. He gathered in all haste a
vast Tartar army, and sent word to Prester John to defend
himself as best as he could. Then Genghis invaded his foe's
territory, and on the beautiful plain of Tenduc met Prester
John's forces in terrible conflict. The battle raged furiously
for two days; at the end of which the invader's victory was
complete. Prester John himself fell dead in the midst of
his host; and Genghis Khan over-ran his kingdom without
resistance. Thus the Tartars had come into the possession
of all China, from the great desert to the eastern seas; and
everywhere, in the region where Marco now was, he saw
the vestiges of their wars and triumphs.

During his expeditions Marco saw and heard much
that was interesting about the Tartars. He found that everywhere he went, they were in the habit of living on the
sides of the mountains in summer and in the sunny and
well, watered valleys in the winter. They could move their
residence thus easily, as the tents they lived in were made

of felt, and being very light, could readily be carried from place to place. They were so superstitious that they always placed the openings of their tents to the South, as to put them in any other way was a bad omen. The Tartar men did nothing but hunt and go to war; their wives did all the home work, the trading, and the cultivating of the fields. They lived principally on milk and the game they brought in from the forests and fields; though sometimes Marco found them feasting on the flesh of camels and even dogs.

These Tartars had each many wives, but they always held the wife they first married in the highest esteem. Husbands and wives were strictly faithful to each other, and a marriage was always the occasion of a great deal of feasting and merry-making. Each Tartar family had an idol of its own, made, curiously enough, of cloth; and very queer-looking things, like rude dolls, did these idols seem to Marco. The idol was placed in a little room apart, and by his side were smaller idols, representing his wife and children. Before the family ate, they smeared the idol's mouth with some fat meat, and lay some pieces of bread at his feet.

The richer Tartars, Marco observed, were often very handsomely attired in robes of silk fringed with gold, and in coats made of many beautiful furs. The soldiers had clubs, swords, and bows and arrows, in the use of the latter of which they were very expert. When they went to war, they wore heavy buffalo cloaks which served as armor.

While Marco was away on one of his jaunts, he one day received a message from his father, saying that the war which had delayed them was now over, and urging him to hasten back to Campicion, that they might proceed on their journey. He therefore hurried back, and as soon as he had arrived, the party once more set out. They had been detained at Campicion no less than a year; no wonder that they were tired of their long wanderings.

The travellers now passed through scenes marked by the ravages of a ferocious war. In some places the villages were entirely laid waste; in others, half-burned cities betrayed the savage nature of the contest. At last they emerged again into a pleasant and thriving region, and soon found themselves in the lovely plain of Tenduc, where, long before, the great battle between Genghis Khan and Prester John had been fought. Here Marco was surprised to learn that most of the inhabitants were Christians; and he saw for himself that they were very industrious, and were prosperous farmers and skilful artisans. This was the country which, it was said, was once upon a time ruled over by two mighty giants, named Gog and Magog. Marco heard with delight that Tenduc was not many days' journey from the place where at last his eyes would be gratified with the sight of Kublai, the great khan. The travellers were already in Cathay, and the end of their long wanderings was near. They had learned that Kublai Khan was at his summer palace at Shandu, in the northern part of his dominions; and they had accordingly directed their course thither. Nicolo knew well that they would be most warmly welcomed when they came into the Tartar sovereign's presence for when he had been in Cathay before, he had found it difficult to get away from the khan's court.

As they approached the goal of their travels, the Venetians passed through a more and more thickly settled country, and larger and richer cities; until one morning they arrived at an imposing place called Cianganor, where were a stately palace and a vast park belonging to the khan. This was only a three day's journey from Shandu; and Nicolo resolved to stay here until he had sent forward a messenger to Kublai Khan to apprize him of their coming, and to receive his reply. They had not long to wait; for within a week their messenger returned, with a numerous and brilliant cavalcade which the khan had dispatched to escort the Venetians to his palace. At the same time, he sent word that he was awaiting their arrival with great impatience.

No time was lost in setting out for Shandu, the road to which lay through a smiling and thickly settled country. On the third day, about noon, they had arrived within sight of the vast palace which served the khan as his summer residence, and beyond which stretched out for miles, the hunting grounds where he enjoyed the rough pastimes of the chase. As the travellers approached nearer, they perceived a great multitude of horsemen coming towards them; and soon one of their escort exclaimed that the khan himself was there. Marco eagerly strained his eyes in the direction of those who were approaching and pretty soon was able to perceive a huge elephant in the midst of the horsemen, upon whose back appeared a glittering canopy of silk and gold. It was indeed the khan, coming out to welcome his guests.

RECEPTION OF THE POLOS BY KUBLAI KHAN

As soon as he was near enough, the khan descended from his elephant, and the Polos and their party leaped from their horses upon the ground. Nicolo, Maffeo and Marco advanced toward the monarch with bowed heads, and fell at his feet. Kublai gently raised the brothers, and warmly embraced one, and then the other.

"Good Venetians," he said, "I am filled with joy to see you. Welcome back to Cathay. You have kept your promise to return, and I am grateful to you. But who," he asked, turning to Marco, "is this comely youth?"

"Sire," replied Nicolo. "He is your majesty's servant, my son."

The khan looked at Marco from head to foot, and advancing to him, smiled very pleasantly.

"Then," said he, "your son is also welcome. I am much pleased with him."

Once more mounting, the three Polos rode by the khan's side until they reached the palace. That evening the khan gave a great feast in honor of the travellers' arrival; and that night, the Polos found themselves luxuriously lodged in some of the best apartments the imperial palace afforded.

CHAPTER VI.

The Imperial Hunting Grounds

IT had taken the Polos almost four long years to reach the hunting grounds of the great khan from Venice. Marco, who was seventeen when he set out from home, was now a tall and slender young man of twenty-one, bronzed by the suns and hardships of many months, and rejoicing in a slight moustache, which imparted a manly appearance to his features.

He had seen many strange sights in the lands through which he had passed; had witnessed many singular peoples, gorgeous shows, and perilous sports. But when he beheld the splendid establishment of Kublai Khan at Shandu, he thought to himself that this far surpassed all that he had before witnessed. Here, at the further end of the world, at the remotest confines of Asia, was a display of riches and magnificent luxury such as, probably, no European potentate, however mighty, could maintain.

It was not long before he had ample opportunities to observe everything in the great summer palace at Shandu and the vast hunting grounds, stretching away for miles over forest, hill and dale, which served as the scene of the hardy recreations of the Tartar monarch. Installed in the palace, and finding himself surrounded on every hand by its lavish decorations and its numberless comforts, he eagerly scanned all the objects about him.

The palace itself was a vast though not very lofty edifice, constructed of marble, porphyry, and other beautiful stones. It comprised long series of spacious halls, and enclosed a number of wide, sunny courts, in the midst of which rare plants flourished and fountains forever played. The walls of the apartments were painted with figures of men, women, beasts and birds; and, however rude these paintings seemed to Venetians, accustomed to the most advanced art the world then knew, their colors were brilliant and gorgeous, and they presented to Marco's eyes a dazzling effect. They much resembled, indeed, the pictures which we now see that come from Japan. Between these pictures, the walls were lavishly gilded, and shone wonderfully. In the great hall was a raised dais, sheltered by a large canopy of the richest cloth; and upon the dais was a gorgeous throne, which seemed ablaze with gold, and upon which the khan sat when, as he often did, he held his court at Shandu.

Besides this main palace there stood, in the park beyond, another palace which was put up when the khan went to Shandu, and was taken down again when he departed from thence to his southern capital. This building was quite as large as the other, but was made of thick, long canes, that grew plentifully in the neighboring jungles. These were cut lengthwise from one knot to the other, and formed the roof; and the structure was supported by stout silken cords. It was, indeed, rather a kind of wooden tent than a building, and was so arranged that it could be taken apart and packed away; and yet, when it was set up, its walls appeared decorated with gay pictures of hunting scenes, which were relieved by broad stripes of gilt. The roof of the edifice was so thickly varnished as to be perfectly water tight.

Surrounding these palaces were the vast hunting grounds devoted to the pastimes of the khan and his pleasure-loving court. They were enclosed by a wall which was no less than sixteen miles around. The tract thus enclosed presented the most attractive variety of Oriental scenery. There were dense forests crowded with huge trees, in which roamed not only stags, deer and wild goats, but lions, tigers, leopards and elephants. There were enchanting dells, through the midst of which flowed sparkling streams and in which the hunters might rest and dine amid their sport. There were broad spaces of lawn and flower-garden, with many fountains playing on the turf and flowers, and lovely groves that gave grateful shelter from the blazing summer sun of Tartary. There were delightful meadows, stretching off from the slopes of verdant hills to the borders of rivers, ponds and lakes and there were carefully-tended parks where, in the open air, the Tartar court held many of its solemn festivals and more joyous merry-makings.

But even all this did not suffice to content the khan in his summer pleasures. Three days' journey away there stood, at Cianganor, yet another palace, whither he retreated when he wearied of the delights of Shandu. This palace was quite as large as the other two, and it had the advantage of being situated on a very broad and beautiful plain, and on the borders of a charming lake. It was here that the khan found the smaller game which it pleased him to hunt when he had got tired of slaughtering tigers and wild goats; for the woods and lake-side about Cianganor abounded in pheasants, partridges and cranes. Marco, when he went with the khan and his train to this retreat, was especially struck with the cranes that he saw there. They were far more beautiful in form and color than those he had seen in Europe. Some were large, and of a dense, glossy black; others were white, with their feathers "full of round gold eyes," like peacocks; yet others were red and black, and others, again, were gray, with red and black heads.

Not far from this palace, in a little valley that descended toward the lake, were a number of small houses, where the khan kept large flocks of partridges. When he went hunting at Cianganor, he usually carried falcons and hawks with him; and many an exciting day did Marco spend there in the exciting sport of hawking.

Sometimes these royal hawking parties comprised an immense number of men, carrying a perfect multitude of hawks and vultures. On more than one occasion, when Marco attended the khan, as many as ten thousand falconers went along, carrying half that number of falcons. When this army of sportsmen reached the hunting ground they dispersed themselves, by twos, over a wide space. One of them, at one end, would then let fly his falcon, which would be watched by the others as it receded, and flew for its prey; and it, with its prey, would be caught by the attendant nearest where they came in conflict. Each falcon had a silver label on its feet, on which was engraved its name and that of its owner; and thus, having done its work, it was duly returned into the right hands again.

The great khan himself set out on these hawking expeditions in splendid array. He always went with four enormous elephants, whose magnificent trappings betrayed the imperial rank of him they bore; and on reaching the hunting ground, he had a square tent, of gold cloth and lions' skins, erected in a convenient place, from an opening in which he witnessed and took part in the sport. When the game was started up, some of the falconers, riding to the royal tent, would cry out, "Sire, the birds are passing;" whereon the khan threw open the side of the tent, let fly one of his favorite hawks, and then, throwing himself back upon his luxurious couch, watched the plunges and whirlings of the birds in the air, as the falcon swooped on its victims.

But exciting as was this sport, that which still more fascinated Marco was the fiercer and more dangerous hunting that he witnessed at Shandu. There the khan possessed a most imposing menagerie of wild beasts, which he used for attacking the ferocious denizens of his forests.

Not far from the palace was a long line of low buildings which, when Marco came to inspect them, proved to be nothing less than enormous cages. On peering within the massive bars, he saw a number of wild animals. There were sleek yellow and black spotted leopards, pacing stealthily and watchfully up and down, and now and then stopping and showing their sharp teeth there were cunning looking lynxes, with their keen, restless eyes; and in some of the cages were animals, the like of which Marco had never before seen. At first he took them for lions. He had never seen a live lion, it is true, but he had seen the bronze effigies of the lions of St. Marc, which stood near the big cathedral at home, and these animals appeared to resemble them. They were not, however, lions, but tigers a beast not then known in Europe. Marco gazed with interest, not unmixed with terror, upon these ferocious creatures, with their smooth striped skins and their savage faces, with which he afterward became familiar in the hunting field. In other cages were stately eagles, sitting solemn and still on their perches, and glaring steadily at their visitor; and in kennels near the cages were many varieties of hunting dogs. Marco was soon to learn that the khan took the tigers out hunting with him and set them upon stags, wild oxen, wild boars and wild goats; and that the eagles were used to hunt animals as large as foxes, and even wolves. A fight between an eagle and a wolf was one which aroused him to the most intense excitement. It was with great interest that, one day, he saw the khan mounted and going to the hunt with a sleek little leopard squatted on the crupper of his horse, apparently as tame and contented as possible. This leopard the khan employed to run down and kill stags and wild deer.

Nothing surprised Marco more than the great establishment of dogs kept by the khan. Two of his nobles, who were brothers, were the keepers of the dogs; and under

them were no less than ten thousand men, who took the
dogs to the hunt. These men were divided into two corps,
one of whom wore yellow costumes, and the other, blue;
and it was a grand sight to see this numerous and brilliant
company set out, on a sunny morning, with thousands of
hounds and mastiffs, growling and barking, leaping about,
and when let loose, running with the greatest speed, while
the trumpets sounded the calls, and the Tartar monarch,
mounted on his elephant, advanced in the midst.

Besides his hunters, the khan had many pet dogs of
every breed, shape, size and color that Asia afforded. Some
of them had been brought from the far north, from the
bleak regions of Siberia; and a few of them were European
dogs, such as Marco was already familiar with. These dogs
were highly trained, and the khan and his court were often
wont to spend long summer afternoons lolling on couches,
or stretched upon the lawn, watching their funny antics.

Sometimes, when the khan went a considerable distance
from his palace in pursuit of the pleasures of which he was
fond, a large number of tents was carried by his numerous attendants; and on reaching a favorable spot, the tents
were pitched by some brawling river, or on a shaded plain,
and thus a canvas city suddenly made its appearance. This
"camping-out" of the Tartar court was on a most elaborate
scale. For the higher nobles an enormous tent was spread,
in which a thousand men were lodged. The khan himself
had a gorgeous pavilion, sustained by columns of cedar
and other perfumed wood, and garnished, inside and
out, by a profusion of lions' and tigers' skins. At the sides

hung ermine and zibelline skins of vast value, elaborately worked with great art and skill. This royal tent, too, was supplied with gilded and painted furniture of the most gaudy description. Divans with huge silk-covered cushions, beds into which one sank almost out of sight, lounges and chairs of downy softness, hangings of the heaviest texture and most brilliant colors, enabled the khan to live in as luxurious comfort in his pleasure camp as at his palace.

Around the royal tent were other smaller tents, only less splendid than itself. Some of these were occupied by his ladies, others by his astronomers, doctors and chief hunters, and still others by his dogs and falcons. A strong guard was posted night and day near the royal tent; and in it, every night, were held feasts in which every delicacy of dish or fruit was partaken of, no matter how distant the camp might be from the nearest city.

All this was so new and strange to Marco, that for the first few months of his stay with the khan he did nothing but gaze and wonder. He seemed to be in a new world; to have been transported from our globe to some distant planet, where every scene and custom were wholly un-familiar. The khan, pleased with his appearance at first, liked Marco more and more as he came to know him better. He indulged the young Venetian in many privileges from which even his own nobles were excluded; learned from him to speak Italian pretty well; and always insisted on his going with the royal party on its expeditions. Marco might roam in the palace or through the hunting grounds as he pleased; the best that the palace afforded was set before him when he dined or supped; and when he went abroad, he could, if he chose, call a guard to attend and protect him.

Sometimes Marco, as well as his father and uncle, was admitted to the royal table itself. The first time that he enjoyed this privilege, he saw a sight which deeply impressed him, and at first completely deceived him. No sooner were the khan and his company fairly seated, than the magicians (who were solemn looking men, with long beards and long black robes) rose and waved their wands; whereupon the cups of wine and milk, intended for the khan, and which were on a table apart, moved as of themselves, and placed themselves before the monarch. Marco found that the Tartars, and even the khan himself, believed that this was done by real magic; but he soon suspected that the cups were moved by mechanical contrivances, secretly arranged by the magicians themselves.

The magicians of the court, indeed, greatly interested Marco. They often dressed in more splendid costumes than the nobles themselves; and they were not only magicians, but priests. The religious festivals of the Tartars were held very frequently, and were attended by much pomp and ceremony. Fireworks, such as Marco had never imagined, were let off at night; and troops of women filled the air with strange, wild songs. The khan was always very anxious that all due respect should be paid to his idols on their feast days; for the magicians threatened him with all sorts of misfortunes, as a result of his neglect to celebrate these occasion and of the wrath of the idols thereat.

Besides the magicians, there was a vast number of monks

in the vicinity of the imperial hunting grounds, whose monasteries crowned the hills and crags in every vicinity. Some of these monks were married, and lived with their families in little huts near the monasteries; but most of them, like the European monks, remained unmarried. They ate nothing but the boiled husks of corn, shaved their heads and beards, wore a very coarse attire, and slept either on rude mats or on the bare ground. Marco was surprised to find an order of men, in distant Cathay, so nearly resembling the monks of his own country.

Marco's first summer in Cathay, amid all these scenes and excitements, passed very rapidly. The month of August was fast drawing to an end; and from what he observed of the movements around him, it was evident that the Tartar court would soon leave Shandu, and proceed to the khan's southern capital. He soon received confirmation of this conjecture; for, one day, the magicians announced to the khan that the 28th of August was near, and reminded him that he must be at Kambalu, his capital, on that day, "to sprinkle the milk of the sacred mares."

On asking a young Tartar noble, who had been very friendly to him, and of whom he had made quite an intimate companion, what this meant, the former replied:

"There is, in the south, a race of sacred mares which are as white as the driven snow. Their milk is also sacred, and must not be drunk by any one who is not of imperial blood. It is said to preserve life and to impart wisdom. Well, on the 28th of August the great khan takes a large quantity of this milk, and sprinkles it in the air, in every direction.

By his so doing the spirits are able to drink in abundance of the sacred beverage; and in their gratitude to the khan, they protect him and all things that are dear to him."

No sooner had the magicians announced the approach of the time to sprinkle the sacred milk, than the khan gave orders to his court to prepare for their return to Kambalu. All became bustle and confusion in the palace and its neighborhood. It was no small task to get ready for a journey of several hundred miles, and to provide, during its progress, for the luxurious travelling of the monarch and his vast train of nobles and ladies; and thousands of servants were busy night and day making the necessary preparations. The khan meanwhile enjoyed for the last times the hunting in his grounds, and made the most of the brief interval that remained.

At last it was announced that everything had been made ready for departure. Provision trains and guards had started on ahead to post themselves at convenient distances on the route; and after a monster feast, in which all the great people of the court took part, the khan set out on his tour southward.

CHAPTER VII.

The Court of the Great Khan

T was a grand sight to see the vast multitude of courtiers, soldiers, nobles, ladies, and attendants, as it crowded the highway as far as eye could reach, and spread itself out over the plain beyond Shandu.

As Marco gazed on the immense procession, including thousands upon thousands of swarthy Tartars, attired in every variety of gay and brilliant costume, it seemed to him as if a great city of people were emptying itself, and had risen bodily to move to a new site. On one side he saw a long train of large elephants, so long that he could not see the end of it in the distance; each elephant adorned with heavy embroidered trappings and lofty palanquins, and some of them bearing huge bales of goods and provisions. Near by was another train, composed entirely of camels and dromedaries, which strode off in their patient, sober way, bearing also their heavy burdens.

Of troops of horses, some mounted by the fierce Tartar cavalry, with their long moustaches, their rude helmets, their huge yataghans, and their long, limber spears, others bearing packages, others dragging heavy wagons, and yet others strode by gorgeously dressed nobles, there seemed to be no end; in the midst of the great multitude was the khan's corps of kennel-keepers, holding dogs in the leash by the dozen; and here and there were to be seen the moving cages containing the khan's big menagerie—his lions and tigers, his leopards and foxes, his eagles, hawks and falcons. The din that arose from this immense number of people was sometimes deafening. The departure was announced by much blowing of shrill trumpets, and by the beating of flat drums; and from the midst of the many groups of women, the ladies and slaves of the khan and his principal courtiers, proceeded the weird songs of Cathay, which had so startled Marco when he first reached the khan's hunting grounds.

He wondered very much how it was that the officers kept so innumerable a host in anything like good order; for he observed that, in spite of the apparent confusion, the vast caravanserai advanced in regular sections, each body of men and women keeping the place in the procession in which it had set out.

In the very midst of his subjects, went, in magnificent state, Kublai Khan himself. He was perched on the back of an enormous white elephant, down whose huge leathery sides hung draperies of cloth of gold and silver, worked with the symbols of the Buddhist faith in many dazzling colors. Above these draperies appeared a splendid pavilion, supported by slender and beautifully carved pillars of sandal-wood and other aromatic woods. It was curtained in the richest silk; above it rose a little dome, plated with silver, and surmounted by many brilliant plumes, that waved and nodded high in the air.

Within the pavilion was a throne which was one blaze of burnished gold, and which was supplied with a large soft cushion, as large and soft as a feather bed. Its arms were carved tiger's heads, the eyes of the tigers being immense emeralds; and upon this throne sat, or rather reclined, the mighty monarch of Cathay. It was a fine opportunity to observe this famous warrior and king. Of middle height and build, Kublai Khan's dark complexion was yet clear and creamy, and on his cheeks a faint flush lent a rich color to his expressive features. His form was perfect in its proportions; he seemed to have been cast in the finest mould of men. He was at once lithe and athletic; strong of muscle, quick and nervous in motion.

His large, dark eyes shone at once with energy and kindliness; his nose, not large and thick as were those of most of his countrymen, was straight and bold. His lips were thick and sensuous, but beautifully outlined, and full of expression. A short, shiny black beard, just tinged with gray, depended from his round chin, and a narrow black moustache adorned his upper lip. In his ears hung long earrings of tear-shaped pearls, and his robe and turban were of the heaviest and glossiest silk.

On a cushion, on one side of the khan, reposed a beautiful young girl, one of the most recent and well beloved of his many wives; while on the other side of the throne, and chained to its leg, sat a small but handsomely spotted leopard, the khan's favorite pet.

All around the elephant that bore the khan, were other

elephants, which carried his wives and principal courtiers, who were being constantly fanned by their dusky slaves with fans made of peacock's feathers, and fastened to long poles that reached from the ground to the palanquins on the elephant's backs. •

The journey from the imperial hunting grounds to Kambalu, the capital of Cathay, occupied several weeks; for the two places were some hundreds of miles apart. The khan and his caravanserai went leisurely, for there was ample time before them. They halted three or four times each day, and timed their progress so as to reach some large town at nightfall. No sooner did they reach a town, than they found every preparation made to receive them. Vast tents were spread, luxurious feasts loaded down long tables within some of them, while in others beds were arranged for the repose of all. The journey thus seemed no hardship at all, but a delightful excursion. The country through which Marco passed was, for the most part, beautiful. Sometimes the caravanserai passed across tedious deserts and plains, or rank and dangerous jungles; but they usually found themselves winding through lovely valleys, with a rich vegetation all about them, and wide spreading trees that afforded a delicious shade from the sun's rays.

As they approached Kambalu, one bright afternoon, the whole population of the capital seemed to empty itself out to receive them. There was a commingling of two vast multitudes. Relatives and friends greeted each other with the wildest demonstrations of delight and as the khan passed by, the people of the city prostrated themselves, all along the road, in his august presence.

Nothing, thought Marco, could exceed the grandeur of the palace in which, by the invitation of the khan, he now took up his quarters. That at Shandu had amazed him; but it seemed insignificant indeed, when he compared it with this noble edifice, which was comprised in a square a mile on each side, and whose walls rose high above all the surrounding houses. These walls themselves supported buildings which, together, composed a part of the imperial abode.

At their four corners were spacious towers, in which were kept the bows, arrows, yataghans and spears, the bridles and saddles, the helmets and breastplates which comprised the khan's implements of war. Midway between these were other towers, which contained the enormous stores needed for the support of the court. In the vast space, a mile square, enclosed within the walls, were several groups of spacious buildings, some used for the wardrobes, others for the plate and other movable articles; while in the midst of these stood the imperial palace itself, its roof rising high above the rest. •

Marco found this palace, in its general appearance, not unlike that at Shandu; but far larger in the size of its apartments, and far more magnificent in its decorations. The hall was reached by a broad flight of porphyry steps; and this room was so long, that it held six thousand persons at its banquet table. Its walls were fairly crusted with gold and silver; and on them were emblazoned enormous figures of dragons, horses, dolphins, tigers, suns and full moons.

The apartments within this palace seemed to Marco fairly innumerable, and all the chambers were as gorgeously decorated as was the hall itself. The roof especially attracted his attention for it was painted red, blue, and green, and so thickly varnished that it glistened in the sun. Quadrangle after quadrangle succeeded each other, in the centre of which spurted fountains, stood basins full of fish, and grew trees of rarest bloom and verdure.

All the surroundings of the palace were fairly delicious. Marco found a large artificial lake a few rods away, upon which barges so painted and gilded as fairly to dazzle him, gayly floated. This lake was alive with the greatest variety of fish, which daily supplied the khan's table. Near the lake rose an artificial hill, perhaps forty feet high, even on every side which the khan had had planted completely over with evergreens that preserved their soft and genial color the year round. This was called "the green mountain," and on its summit was the prettiest pavilion imaginable, whence a view of all the surrounding country might be enjoyed. It was one of the khan's pet hobbies to cover this eminence with the rarest trees, which he caused to be brought thither from the remotest parts of Tartary and planted.

"How my brother Maffeo and my uncle Marco would wonder to see all this splendor!" mused Marco. "When I get home, and tell them about it, they will not believe me."

The palace stood on the banks of a river; and it was on the other bank of this river that the city of Kambalu (which means, "city of the khan") stood. It was, Marco saw, a large city, some twenty-four miles around, and built regularly in squares; and it stood on or near the site which the great Chinese city of Pekin now occupies. It was entirely sur-rounded by a thick and lofty earthen wall, through which, on the several sides, twelve gates gave admission to the streets.

On either side of these gates were square towers, which were always filled with heavily-armed troops. The streets were really broad, straight avenues, and were lined with wide-spreading trees; and along them were to be seen many fine palaces and temples. Marco saw a very high build-ing in the very centre of the city, on which was a steeple containing a large bell. This bell, he learned, was rung at nightfall three times; this was a signal that the great gates were closed, and that no one could enter or go out of the city until the next day.

Kambalu was a very busy place. It was full of rich mer-chants, who drove a thriving trade, and its bazaars were every day crowded with eager traders dealing in every imaginable kind of wares. From India came to the bazaar stalls precious stones and rich fabrics, and from the Aus-tralasian islands delicious spices and fruits; while Cathay itself supplied them with an abundance of food and cloths. The suburbs of the city stretched away over the hills be-yond the walls as far as eye could reach on either side, and Marco's head ached when he tried to guess how large the population of Kambalu and its vicinity could be.

Marco had not long been at Kambalu, before he learned that the khan had a large number of wives. Of these four were held in higher honor than the rest, and were called

"Empresses." Each of these empresses was entitled to take the khan's name, and each had a separate court of her own, with a palace all to herself. Each empress was attended by no less than ten thousand persons, among whom were three hundred of the loveliest maidens of Cathay. It was a great honor to belong to an empress's court, and all the young girls of the country were anxious to be chosen among this band. By his four empresses, the khan had twenty-two sons, and by his other wives, no less than twenty-five more; and this numerous family lived, one and all, in the greatest splendor and state.

The khan's court, as Marco had seen it at Shandu, was as nothing compared with the court he held at Kambalu. He was constantly guarded by twelve thousand horsemen. After one body of horsemen had served him three days and three nights, they were replaced by another body of the same number; and wherever the khan went, he was attended by this military array.

Marco marvelled at nothing more than at the magnificent feasts which the khan gave on the occasion of an imperial or religious festival. The great banqueting hall of the palace served as the scene of these feasts. At these times, the monarch himself sat at a table at one end of the hall, raised on a dais high above the rest, facing the South. On his left sat his favorite wife, and on his right, his sons and nephews. On a lower platform were stationed the great nobles of the state with their wives, and lower down still, on the floor, were seated the lower dignitaries of Kublai's court. In the very centre of the hall, between the long rows of groaning tables, stood an immense basin of solid gold, and on either side two smaller ones, all filled to overflowing with the choicest wine; and from thence the attendants took the beverage, in flagons, to the feasters.

Two guards, of lofty stature, were stationed at each door of the banqueting hall, with heavy staves. These saw to it that no one who entered or went out touched the threshold; for this was a serious offence in a royal apartment.

Marco observed that those who waited upon the khan and his family, who were nobles of high degree, had their mouths closely wrapped up in silk and gold towels; and soon learned that this was to keep them from breathing upon the dishes destined for the imperial palate. As soon as the khan raised his goblet to drink, the trumpets and drums made a great noise in every part of the hall, and the nobles, leaving their chairs, fell all at once on their knees and raised their hands, in a sort of supplicating attitude, above their heads; and this happened every time the khan quaffed his wine.

While the feast was thus going forward in the great hall, multitudes were eating and drinking to their hearts' content in the smaller apartments surrounding it. In all, it was said that forty thousand people feasted at once within the palace walls. Many of these were nobles or merchants who came from distant parts of the empire, and who had brought costly gifts to the khan.

The eating and drinking over, the tables were cleared and moved aside, the vast company gathered in a semi-circle on the floor, a lofty throne was placed for the khan on the dais, and forthwith in came a host of dancers, singers, magicians, and jugglers; who, in the open space below the monarch, entertained the multitude with the exhibition of their various talents. Marco was especially struck with the jugglers, who performed seemingly impossible feats, and tumbled about greatly to the risk, as he thought, of breaking their necks.

Among the chief festivals that took place at court, were those which celebrated the khan's birthday, and the incoming of the new year, which, in Cathay, began in February. On his birthday, the khan was wont to array himself in a robe of beaten gold, and all his court wore their most gorgeous apparel. The feast was preceded by a solemn ceremony in the principal temple; and after this, presents were offered to the khan by a multitude of his subjects, who came from every part of the country; and also by neighboring princes.

A still more splendid festival was that called the "White Feast," which ushered in the new year. On that day the entire population of the khan's empire attired themselves in white, from head to foot. It was customary on this occasion also to offer gifts to the monarch; indeed, these occasions for making him presents came very often, and served to enrich him beyond calculation. On New Year's day, the presents usually consisted of gold and silver ornaments, rare gems, and costly white cloths, white horses, camels, and elephants, these animals also bearing on their backs boxes and packages of presents, and being habited in the richest apparel.

The ceremony of receiving these offerings, and of celebrating the day, was a most imposing one. The khan and all his court repaired in splendid attire to the great hall of the palace, and ranged themselves in order of rank around the sides. As soon as all had occupied their places, a high priest advanced in the centre and said, in a loud voice, "Kneel and adore!" whereupon all fell upon their knees, struck their foreheads with their hands, and turning to the khan, rendered him homage as if he were a god. Then the crowd advanced to an altar, where the priest poured out incense in the khan's honor.

This ceremony over, the khan, followed by the rest, went out upon the flight of steps leading up to the principal portal of the palace; and as he stood there, beneath a glittering canopy, fanned by peacock fans, and the centre of a dazzling galaxy of silk and jewels, the elephants, camels and horses that bore his innumerable presents passed by in slow procession. All the animals were taught to kneel when they came opposite the khan; and it took several hours for the long train, bearing its countless treasures, to pass.

After this the banquet took place; and on New Year's night, every one at the khan's court felt at liberty to become intoxicated, and to indulge in such wild capers as the wine inspired them to commit. The wine thus drunk was seasoned with rice and rich spices, and was very strong.

At all these festivals and merry-makings, the Polos were not only permitted to be present, but were honored with places in the midst of the nobles. The khan's favor, which was fully and openly bestowed upon the Venetian strangers, served to procure them the good will and friendship of his courtiers.

All this while Marco was learning what seemed to him the endless language of Cathay. He found it a great deal harder than French, which he had studied as a boy at home; but in due time he found that he could converse quite easily with his Tartar companions, and heard every day something new and strange about the land in which he was sojourning.

CHAPTER VIII.

Marco Polo Among the Tartars

BEFORE Marco had lived in the khan's palace a year, he had become quite used to his novel surroundings; and felt as much at home as he could anywhere outside of his native Italy. As soon as he learned the language so as to talk readily, he learned a great deal that was very curious about Cathay. He was never tired of asking questions, and he found many learned men about the court who were very willing to satisfy his curiosity.

He had now thrown aside his Venetian attire, and, like his father and uncle, wore the costume which was imposed upon him by Tartar custom; and very oddly he looked, in loose tunic, small turban, and turned-up shoes, his complexion being many shades lighter than that of the dusky faces around him. He had adopted, also, the Tartar ways of living; and instead of keeping himself apart, made himself one among the courtiers.

The more he saw of Kublai Khan, and the more he learned of his method of governing his vast empire, the more ardently did he admire that energetic and kindly monarch. He observed that whenever there was a great storm, or flood, or other calamity, the khan sent mes-

sengers into the districts where it had occurred, to find
out if the crops had been destroyed; and if they had been,
the khan not only relieved the sufferers of their taxes for
the year, but distributed food among them out of his own
abundant stores.

The khan, in times of plenty, always caused his store-
houses to be filled full of grain and when a period of scarcity
occurred, he ordered this grain to be sold to the common-
folk at a third or a fourth of its cost. The poor people of
Kambalu were constantly fed from the khan's generous
bounty; even the humblest beggar was not turned away
empty from the palace doors. Not only did the khan thus
provide the hungry with food, but the ragged with cloth-
ing. Of the silk, hemp, and wool which he collected as a
part of the tributes due him, he caused cloths to be made
in a building within the palace walls; and these cloths
were turned into comfortable garments, and given freely
to those who stood in need of them. The good monarch
also took care that there should be spacious highways
leading from every part of his dominions to the capital.
Nor was he content with merely constructing these roads;
he caused them to be planted, on either side, with tall
trees, which served at once to afford the tired traveller a
grateful shade on his way, and to guide him aright to his
destination. When the soil was such that trees could not
be planted, the khan caused mile-stones to be erected at
convenient intervals. On these highroads, at distances of
five-and-twenty miles, were stationed a kind of post houses,
to serve as resting-places both for the khan's messengers,

and for travellers. These houses were often spacious and luxuriously furnished, and many horses were kept in the stables, so as to be ready for use at any moment.

The khan, indeed, had no need to fear that his treasure would ever become exhausted; for he had the power, and freely used it, to manufacture as much money as he chose. This he did with the rind beneath the bark of a certain tree. This was cut up into small strips, and stamped with the royal seal; and thus the khan had an ample supply of funds. This was, perhaps, the earliest known employment of paper money. It surprised Marco very much to see the Tartars burning lumps of "blackstone," instead of wood, in their fire-places; for he had never seen or heard of coal in Europe.

Nothing about the court was more interesting to Marco than the many astrologers and magicians whom he saw there, and who were held in high honor by the khan and all his courtiers. These grave men, who always wore very long beards and had wise, solemn countenances, were supported at the khan's expense, and were constantly engaged in the exercise of their mysterious arts. They studied the stars, and had many curious instruments for this purpose; and from the positions and course of the heavenly bodies, they foretold the weather and many other events. When they made their prophecies, these were written down on small tablets, and sold to all who wished to peer into the future. When a noble courtier was going to a distance, and desired to know whether he would be overtaken by storms, or would succeed in the object of his journey, he

went to an astrologer to be informed, and paid him roundly
for his service.

Marco often attended the religious rites in the temples,
and noted with curiosity the religious customs of the
people. Each Tartar had, he observed, a small tablet fixed
in the wall of one of his rooms, with the name of Buddha
engraved upon it in large letters. To this tablet he and his
family prayed every morning. They prostrated themselves
on the ground, raised their hands, frantically beat their
foreheads, and then burned incense in honor of their
god. On the floor below the tablet, stood a small statue
of an inferior god, who was supposed to have a care of
the earthly affairs of Buddha's worshippers, and to whom
prayers were offered for good weather, full crops, and
health. The Tartars believed that as soon as a man died,
his soul inhabited a new body; that a poor man who had
been good during this life, would be reborn a gentleman,
or perhaps a noble; but that on the other hand a man of
rank who had been wicked would, after death, become a
peasant, and afterwards a dog or a wolf.

The more Marco saw of the Tartars the more he respected and liked them. He was pleased with their polite
and gentle manners; he was attracted by their agreeable,
smiling faces; he noticed with what cleanliness and care
they ate; and he observed that children invariably treated
their parents with reverence and humility, and that the
punishment of a child who rebelled against parental authority was very severe.

The khan was treated by his subjects with a respect and

awe which passed the bounds of servility. When any one came within half a mile of where the khan was, he at once assumed a very sober face, advanced slowly and softly, and talked in a subdued voice; and on reaching the portal of the palace, proceeded to produce from a pocket a pair of soft leather buskins, with which he replaced his shoes. On entering the royal presence, he fell upon the carpet, and did not lift his head until he had received the khan's permission to do so.

But the time was soon to come when Marco must abandon the idle and luxurious life he had so long led, and to engage in active and perilous service for the khan. Everything about the court and city had amused and interested him, and the days had passed quickly amid so many strange scenes and so many brilliant shows and attractions. He could scarcely believe in the rapid passage of time; and he almost forgot that his presence in Cathay was for more serious purposes than to saunter and dream among those beautiful and be-wildering surroundings. Yet, when the moment arrived for him to arouse himself, to enter upon active pursuits, and do something to show his gratitude for all the khan's generosity, hospitality and kindness, he was by no means sorry; for Marco had an adventurous disposition, and was happiest when engaged in some stirring task.

 ✦ One afternoon, when he was lolling in his apartment, an attendant entered and summoned Marco into the khan's presence. Kublai was reposing by a fountain in one of the shady courtyards of the palace. Dark-visaged slaves were fanning him with peacock fans, as the monarch reclined on soft pillows, and quaffed, every now and then, a cooling beverage from a golden goblet. By his side lay, in languid attitude, two of his beautiful young wives, attired in light but exceedingly rich costumes, their ears, necks and arms sparkling with many gems. Around the khan stood a group of courtiers and attendants; while in the corners of the courtyard, gigantic and fierce-featured guards watched over his safety.

Marco approached and made the usual humble obeisance to the monarch. Kublai, raising himself on his elbow, motioned to Marco to come nearer and stand by him; for he said he had something to say to him.

"Venetian," began Kublai, "I have made you very welcome at my court, and have found pleasure in your presence. Your countenance was agreeable to my eyes when I first saw you; and since, your conduct has been such as to win my confidence and esteem. I trust you, and believe that you are devoted to me. Is it not so?"

Marco replied that he longed for an occasion to show the khan how grateful he was for all that the khan had done for him.

"Such an occasion has now arisen," continued the khan. "There is grave business to be done in my western and southern provinces. They are disturbed, and the people do not understand my fatherly care over them. I must send thither some one who will reason with them, and explain my proceedings; who will persuade them to be submissive, and assure them that they may be certain of justice and protection. This task, Venetian, I have marked out for you."

"Nothing," declared Marco, "would please me better than to undertake it. I thank your majesty for the confidence you thus repose in me."

"Your journey will be long, and it may be perilous. My subjects in those distant portions of my empire are not easily governed. Sometimes they break out into rebellion. Besides, the mountains are full of robbers, who dare to attack even my royal messengers. But you are a brave and active youth, and danger has no terrors for you. You shall go well guarded; shall give orders that you are attended as the chosen envoy of the great khan should be."

Marco was far from dismayed by the prospect before him. Now that it was decided upon, he became impatient to enter on his travels, and encounter the possible perils of which the khan had spoken. His father was at first loth to have him go. He feared lest he should never see his young son again. But Nicolo knew that Kublai Khan's will was law; and that, however kind he might be on ordinary occasions, he was very resolute that his will, when expressed, should be obeyed at once, and without a murmur.

In no long time the preparations for Marco's setting out were complete. He was to be attended by a considerable guard of soldiers, armed to the teeth; and also by a large train of attendants, as an indication of his rank and his position near the khan.

The day of departure came; and Marco, arrayed in Tartar costume, his belt well armed with sword and daggers, and his horse fresh and sleek from the royal stables, bade the khan adieu in the midst of his court. He received his

last instructions from one of the principal ministers, and
then retired to his father's apartment to embrace Nicolo
and Maffeo for the last time. This touching interview over,
he mounted his horse, and accompanied by his guard .and
attendants, emerged from the palace gate, crossed the
river, and wended his way leisurely through the spacious
avenues of Kambalu.

Soon the open country beyond the suburbs was reached,
and now Marco pushed forward more rapidly. When he
had gone about ten miles he came to a river, much wider
and more rapid than that which flowed beneath the palace
wall. On approaching the banks, he espied before him the
finest bridge he had ever seen. It was built of stone, and
had four-and-twenty arches supported by massive piers
imbedded in the stream. At one end was a lofty column
of marble, around the foot of which were several skilfully
carved figures of lions. As he rode across the bridge, Marco
found that ten horsemen could easily go abreast upon it.
In spite of all that he had already seen in Cathay, Marco
was surprised to find there as splendid a work of art as
this bridge really was.

Continuing his journey, Marco found himself passing
through a rich and thriving country, the soil of which
was fruitful, the landscapes charming, and the people
industrious and busy. He reached towns and villages all
alive with bazaars, and silk and linen factories; he passed
broad fields of waving grain, and beneath avenues of trees
which stretched far away over the hills. On eminences here
and there he espied quite stately castles, guarded by tow-

ers and high walls, just as were the castles he used to see about Venice; and vineyards crept up the slopes to their foundations. Once in a while Marco came upon very large cities, teeming with dense populations, and all alive with manufacture and trade processions of camels and carts going in and out the lofty gateways, and many temples rising high above the mass of dwellings. In the bazaars great fairs were being held; and Marco could not but remark how intelligent and shrewd this race of Tartar merchants seemed. He seized every occasion to talk both with merchants and the native soothsayers, and with the landlords of the inns where he sojourned. He heard accounts of the country through which he was passing, the manners and customs of the people, and, as well, many anecdotes of the events which had taken place in the various neighborhoods.

One afternoon he stopped at a large town called Pianfu, and was enjoying his ease after supper and talking with one of the local gossips. On a hill some two miles distant he observed a very spacious and hoary castle. He asked his companion what castle it was.

"That is the castle of Cayafu," was the reply "and there is an interesting story about a good king who once dwelt there."

Marco was fond of listening to the stories with which all Tartar minds seemed stored, and begged his companion to tell that of Cayafu.

"A long time ago," said the native, "the king of this region, whose name was Dor, had a war with the famous Prester John. The country was invaded by Prester John, but

Dor so stoutly entrenched himself that his enemy could not get at him. Prester John was exceedingly vexed, for he supposed that it would be the easiest matter in the world to conquer Dor; and did not know what to do. Seven of his servants, seeing their master's anger, went to him and told him that, if he chose, they would bring Dor into his tent alive. Prester John listened to them incredulously, but gave them permission to attempt the feat which they proposed. They disguised themselves and got access to Dors camp. Presenting themselves before the king, they offered him their services. Dor received them with a hearty welcome, and gave them posts immediately about his person. He soon became attached to them, and learned to trust them completely. The traitors watched and waited for their opportunity. After a while, it came. Dor set out one day on a short excursion beyond his camp; and with him went these seven men. The party crossed a wide river and entered a dense forest. Perceiving that the king was now separated from the main body of his followers, the villains fell upon the few that remained, stretched one after another dead on the ground, and rudely seized their benefactor.

"'What means this, my children?' exclaimed Dor, amazed. 'What would you do with me? How have I offended you?'

"'We are going to take you to our master—Prester John!'

"Dor, on hearing this, covered his face with his hands and exclaimed: 'How have I been deceived! Why, my children, have I not welcomed and honored you like brothers? And will you, like traitors, give me up to my bitterest foe?'

They said nothing in reply, but putting him bound

upon a horse, hurriedly cleared the forest, and galloped to Prester John's camp as fast as they could go. Prester John was as surprised as he was delighted to see his enemy in his power at last. Turning to him roughly, he exclaimed: "'Well, you are caught at last. Now confess that you are not equal to making war with me.'

"Dor bowed with humility and replied:

"'I know well, sire, that I am not as strong as you. I repent of having taken up arms against you, and in future I will act as your faithful friend.'

"Prester John, though a stout warrior, was not obdurate of heart. On hearing these gentle words fall from his royal prisoner's lips, he arose and embraced him.

"'Be of good cheer, brother,' said he; 'I will not humiliate you any further, but will give you my esteem and friendship.'

"Whereupon Prester John provided Dor with a splendid escort of cavalry, and after having feasted him in a manner worthy of a king, sent him rejoicing back to the castle of Cayafu. From that time Dor and Prester John were the best of friends, and fought side by side in many a furious battle with their common foes."

Marco was deeply interested in this story, and thought it sounded very much like the stories of what sometimes had happened to European kings.

CHAPTER IX.

Marco Polo's Travels in Cathay

AFTER leaving Pianfu Marco travelled steadily west-ward, always seeing something new and curious that deeply impressed itself on his memory. He was surprised at the great size of many of the rivers he crossed, some of which far exceeded in width any he had ever seen in Europe, and which could not be spanned by bridges. When he came to such a stream, he and his train were transported to the further bank on large rafts and barges.

He was especially struck, too, by the size, numbers and splendid plumage of the birds which peopled the Tartar forests, and the plenteous and luscious fruit that grew in the river valleys. Sometimes his road led by zig-zags to the summits of lofty mountains, whence he had fine views of all the country round, and where were spacious inns and royal houses wherein he rested. One bridge that he crossed was constructed wholly of marble, and upon it were long ranges of shops, where a lively trade was going on. This much reminded him of the Rialto, at home in Venice.

At last, after travelling many weeks, he reached the im-portant province of Thibet. As he crossed the borders of this country, he found himself constantly in danger from the bold and barbarous brigands that found safe retreats in its mountain fastnesses. More than once Marco and his companions had to fight these fierce robbers for their lives. As an envoy of the khan, Marco would have been a rich prize; and the treasure he carried with him, to be given as presents to the vassal kings of the khan, would have been no despicable booty. But every time that he encountered the Thibet robbers he repulsed them, and got off with a few slight wounds which soon healed.

Marco was very much struck with the wealth and rich productions as well as the picturesque aspect of Thibet. He found gold very plenty, so plenty that many of the commonest people wore golden ornaments on their arms and around their necks. Cinnamon was one of the most valuable resources of the country; and the women displayed a great deal of coral on their persons. Thibet was full of wizards and astrologers; but Marco thought them, unlike those of Kambalu, wicked men, who served rather the devil than mankind.

He saw many very large dogs in the country, which seemed to him as big as donkeys, and which were excellent hunters; and he was amazed at the height to which the canes grew in the jungles. These canes were used by caravans who passed through the jungles at night, to make fires with, and thus to keep off the lions, tigers, and bears that prowled in the dark, dismal swamps.

There was a long tract of country in Thibet which was uninhabited; and Marco and his companions were obliged to take enough food with them to last until they had crossed this tract. Every night they camped in the dreary solitude, making great roaring fires of the gigantic canes. On reaching the limit of this waste, Marco found a country that was inhabited, indeed, but by a degraded and wicked people, who robbed every one who came into their neighborhood without scruple, and lived on the fruits and on what game they could procure in the woods. They used lumps of salt as money, and clad themselves in the skins of wild beasts and in the coarsest cloths. Marco saw cinnamon, cloves, and ginger growing in this region, and examined them with eager curiosity.

On crossing the wide river which formed the frontier of Thibet, Marco reached a kingdom ruled over by one of the great khan's sons. Here again he saw plenty and prosperity, noble castles and thriving cities. He paid a visit to the king, the khan's son, from whom he received a very gracious welcome, and who entertained him with much honor in his palace.

Marco was glad to once more find himself in a land which appeared thrifty and civilized. The people seemed to him more like those of Kambalu than any he had seen; and he narrowly observed their various customs and industries. He saw a great deal of grain and rice growing, and noticed that here the money was made of a kind of porcelain, taken from the sea. Vast quantities of salt were dug from pits near the principal city; and not far off there was a great lake, a hundred miles long, from which an abundance of fish of many kinds were taken. The people ate their meat and fish raw in garlic sauce.

While Marco was in this country, he enjoyed a strange sort of sport—that of snake-hunting. It appeared that the region abounded in huge reptiles, some of them twenty or more feet long, with heads shaped like a loaf of bread, and big mouths wide enough to swallow a man. These snakes lay, in the daytime, in underground caves, where it was dark and slimy; crawling forth at night in search of prey, and to drink in the rivers and ponds. They thus made long tracks in the sand.

Marco set out, late one afternoon, with a party of snake-hunters, and soon came to a place where these tracks were visible.

Some of the natives at once set to work, fixed a kind of trap across the tracks, and covered it all over with sand. They then lay in wait till a snake should squirm out of his cavern, and make his way toward the neighboring river. Presently one was seen, slipping rapidly along through the sand, straight towards the spot where the trap was concealed. In another moment the trap had caught his huge body. The snake's head rose high in air, his fangs shot out, and a sharp hissing noise was heard. The natives rushed up, and found that the teeth of the trap had nearly severed the reptile in two; and a few blows soon settled him. The party returned in triumph, and Marco was delighted to have seen so novel a sport.

The huge snake's gall bladder was taken out and, on asking why this was done, Marco learned that it was an infallible remedy for the bite of a mad dog. The snake's body was then cut up, and sold for food; the people regarding it as a very delicate and palatable dish.

Marco saw in this land many magnificent horses, in which the people took great pride. The men were very skilful horsemen, and always went to the hunt or to battle astride of their steeds. Marco was very much pleased when, on parting from the king, the latter presented him with several of the finest of these horses.

The next province which Marco reached seemed to him a very curious place, so strange were the manners and customs of its people. He perceived that the first man and woman whom he met on the road had their teeth completely covered with plates of gold; and he soon found that this was the general custom. The money of this people consisted both of porcelain, gold, and silver. They had no idols or temples, but each family worshipped its chief as a god. Nor did they have any doctors; but when any one was ill, they sent for a magician, who performed incantations over the invalid, and danced about and howled in the most dismal manner.

Their way of making a bargain struck Marco as singular. The two traders cut a piece of wood into two equal halves, and each took one of the halves and after the bargain had been completed, and the money paid over, he who paid the money also delivered up his piece of the wood. Another strange custom was this. When a woman had given birth to a child, instead of remaining in bed and tending it, her husband took her place, while she went about her household work; and the man staid in bed with the child forty days, at the end of which period he rose, and entertained his relatives and friends with a bounteous feast. From this place, which was situated high among the mountains, Marco began what was called "the great descent." He went down hill for nearly three days, descending from the mountains into the valley below. This valley had scarcely a human habitation. It was nearly covered with dense forests, where roamed elephants, leopards, and rhinoceroses, at will. To cross these forests was a perilous task; happily a good road led through them, and Marco found convenient openings at night where to fix his camp.

But often, as he lay on his rude bed made of branches, while the flames of the big fire his attendants had built flickered through the opening of his tent, he heard the terrible roar of the wild beasts, which seemed only a few feet off. He half expected to feel their hot breath against his cheek, and their teeth burying themselves in his flesh. The fires proved, however, an effectual defence; and ere many days the party emerged safe and sound from the depths of the dreadful forest into the open country again.

Marco was delighted to find, just beyond, a fine and populous city, where he could see the faces of men once more, and repose in a comfortable bed. The most remarkable thing he observed in the city was a magnificent tomb, erected in honor of one of its kings. Above the tomb were two towers, twenty feet high, one of silver, and the other of gold; at their summits were round cupolas hung with golden bells, which tinkled merrily whenever they were stirred by the breeze.

The further Marco penetrated to the westward, the more numerous and dangerous did he find the wild beasts that infested the country. But wherever they were most to be dreaded, the natives were most skilful in hunting and destroying them. In one place Marco saw a lion-hunt which greatly excited him. The party went out on horseback, carrying a pack of large, ferocious, but well-trained dogs. As soon as they found a lion, prowling and roaring on the edge of the jungle, the dogs were unleashed, and rushed for the lion with loud, fierce barks. Dodging around his shaggy head, they quick as lightning pounced upon his hind legs and thighs, into which they fixed their long sharp teeth. The lion whirled around to seize them; but the dogs were always too quick for him, and kept their grip grimly on the hind parts of his body. Then the lion ran howling to a large tree, against which he set his back. But this was of no avail, for the dogs kept their hold, and made him keep turning round and round in a circle. Meanwhile the hunters pierced him through and through with arrows and javelins in front, until he fell dead at their feet.

In course of time Marco came to the vast city of Nankin, which is to-day second in size to the Chinese capital of Pekin. He found it a very busy place, all alive with manufactures, and the country round about exceedingly fruitful. He did not stay at Nankin long, however, but pressed on still westward.

All this time he was faithfully fulfilling the errand with which Kublai Khan entrusted him. Whenever he reached a province where it was necessary to reconcile the chiefs or

LION HUNTING IN CATHAY

the people to the khan, Marco used his persuasions, accompanied by lavish presents; and he so favorably impressed the chiefs everywhere, that he was usually successful in his aim. Now and then he found a province which could not be persuaded to yield to the khan's wishes; and such places Marco left to be subdued by force of arms.

Marco had not for many a long month set eyes upon the sea; and born, as he had been, on the sea coast, he had always been fond of the briny deep. He was much rejoiced, therefore, when in the course of his wanderings he reached one of the Tartar seaports, and could gaze out once more over the expanse of waters. This port was a very thriving one; Marco thought there must have been no less than five thousand craft in its harbor; certainly there was a perfect forest of lateen sails and curious sloops and brigs. It was at the mouth of a very broad and deep river, whose waters were in their turn fairly covered with vessels of all kinds, which were drawn through the water with ropes made of a limber sort of cane.

Not long after leaving this seaport and proceeding inland again, Marco came to a city the size and beauty of which, although he had already seen many beautiful cities, fairly astonished him. This was called Kinsai, or the chief city, and was the same place as that now called Hang-chou-fou. He was told, and could almost believe it, that the walls around Kinsai were no less than one hundred miles in circumference; as he neared the gates, the buildings stretched out on every side as far as the eye could reach, presenting the same idea of vastness which London now does to the eyes of the approaching traveller. He found it harder to believe that there were at least twelve thousand bridges within the limits of the city, all built of stone, beneath many of which ships of the largest size could pass.

As he passed through the streets of Kinsai, he wondered more and more at the great wealth and extreme beauty and activity of the place. Many trades were evidently pursued there; for great warehouses and factories covered block after block, and long lines of bazaars bordered the side-walks, or ran though the centre of the broad avenues; while palatial residences, belonging to the merchants, crowned the hills above the business quarter.

Marco, a comely young man of twenty-three or four, could not fail to remark that the women of Kinsai were "of angelic beauty," and that in their apparel they were as elegant and showy as the ladies of the European courts. The men were tall and stalwart, and full of vigor and enterprise in their movements. The streets, in whatever direction Marco turned, were well paved with large stones and he observed, at brief intervals, large square buildings which, he learned, were the public baths. Of these he was told there were no less than four thousand in the city, in each of which a hundred people could bathe at once; and now Marco was at no loss to account for the very neat appearance that all the natives made. Marco had the curiosity, one day soon after reaching Kinsai, to go into one of these large bath-houses. He found a wide square pool of clear, cold water in the centre, with broad flights of stone steps leading down into it; and there was a crowd of forty or fifty men, women and children, of all ages and sizes, with only a cloth band about their waists, floundering about in the water, and evidently much enjoying themselves.

In the very centre of the city Marco found the royal palace, which had been occupied by the ancient kings of the country before it was conquered by Kublai Khan. It was scarcely less magnificent than Kublai's palace itself. Like the latter, it was surrounded by vast, high walls; and between these walls were orchards, lawns, parks, sparkling fountains, glossy little lakes, and artificial hillocks thickly planted with rare trees and shrubs. The great hall of the palace was decorated in gold and azure, and covered with pictures of beasts, birds, knights, beautiful women, and enchanting landscapes. Other buildings stood around the palace, and in all, Marco was told, there was ample room to seat ten thousand men at table. In the palace were no less than one thousand bed chambers.

Not far from this right royal edifice was a high mound, on which was placed a large wooden table; and upon this, when there was a fire in any part of the city, a man struck heavy blows with a hammer, which resounded sharply to a considerable distance. In another part of the city was a large stone tower, whither people whose houses were on fire carried their household effects for safe-keeping, until they could procure a new abode.

Marco made quite a long stay at Kinsai, for it was by far the most important place he was to visit in the western portion of the khan's dominions. Many of the customs of the people interested and amused him. It appeared that every dweller in the city caused his own name and those of his wife, children and servants, to be written on his front door; and whenever a child was born, his or her name was added. When any one of the family died, the name of the deceased was erased from the door. There was a beautiful lake at a short distance out of Kinsai, in which were two very picturesque islands. On one of these stood a splendid palace; and whenever a couple of the higher class were married, they always went to this island palace, with their relations and friends, there to celebrate, amid lovely scenes and on embowered terraces overlooking the lake, their wedding feast. At funerals, the friends of the departed made images of horses, camels, cloths, money, and other things that mortals enjoy on earth, out of stiff cards; and when the funeral pyre was lighted, threw these images into the flames, saying that in the other world the deceased one would enjoy the realities which these represented.

CHAPTER X.

Marco Polo's Return

ARCO was very reluctant to leave Kinsai. Every day that he tarried there, he saw something new and curious; he thought it a far more interesting city than Kambalu. Attended by one or two of the Tartars who had accompanied him on his journey, and by an old merchant whom he had attached to him, he went about the streets, marvelling at the vastness of the place and its population, at the immense collection of goods displayed in the warehouses and shops, and especially at the great public works, comforts and conveniences, which gave evidence of a civilization in many respects as high as that of Europe itself.

He found ten or twelve vast squares, half a mile long, succeeding each other in regular order and in a straight line, from one end of the city to the other. On these squares were lofty warehouses, filled to overflowing with goods from India and Arabia, from Africa, Java and Ceylon. Parallel to this series of squares ran a broad canal, crossed, at the intersection of the streets, by dainty little bridges; and on either side of the canal, rows of stone warehouses.

There were certain days in the week when these business quarters were thronged by thousands of merchants from every Eastern clime, and in all the picturesque costumes of the Orient. In the markets Marco saw the greatest variety of game and fruit. There were partridges and pheasants, fowl, ducks and geese. On the stalls of the fruiterers were immense pears, some of which seemed to Marco to weigh ten pounds, and which were delicious to eat; large luscious peaches, yellow and white; and grapes of many hues and flavors.

Each avocation, rank and profession of the people seemed to have a quarter of its own in which to reside. In one quarter lived, in spacious mansions often richly frescoed on the exterior, the prosperous merchants. There were streets on which you could find no one but astrologers and seers; others devoted to doctors and teachers; yet others where all the residents were artisans. Many of the wealthier mansions had lovely gardens, with marble fountains and blooming flower beds attached to them. The interiors displayed very rich carvings, and luxurious furniture.

The lake which has been spoken of, where the wedding parties of the rich and noble were held, was full of pretty barges with banners and streamers, which, on pleasant afternoons, fairly dotted its placid waters, crowded with gay pleasure-seekers. They were pushed along by means of long poles; and each barge had its elegantly fitted cabin, with every arrangement for eating and drinking. Sailing in these barges was, indeed, the favorite amusement of the people after the labors of the day were over. Another pastime was driving along the spacious shady avenues in their handsome carriages, which were long, covered at the top, and supplied with elegant silk curtains and cushions. No European dame, however high her degree, would have disdained to ride in one of these luxurious conveyances.

Indeed, Marco found that the people of Kinsai liked very much the same recreations as did the Venetians. What with boating, driving, and sauntering in beautiful gardens, where they drank tea and listened to music, their habits of pleasure closely resembled those of his own countrymen.

The people themselves seemed to him not only highly civilized, but very amiable and agreeable. They lived peaceably, and seemed to hate disturbance and war; and the only class generally disliked in the city were the royal guard placed there by the khan, who kept careful watch over the walls and the palace, and also acted as policemen. The people did not even go armed, and seemed to have but little knowledge of the use of warlike weapons. Their business dealings with each other were frank and honest, and they treated each other with a familiar courtesy very pleasing to see. The men held their wives in high respect, and confided implicitly in them; and all strangers who came to Kinsai were received with the most generous and genial hospitality.

Ruling over Kinsai, before the conquest of the khan, had been a native king, named Facfur. He lived in gorgeous style in the palace, and had had everything for his enjoyment that heart could wish. In the inner part of the palace, beyond the sight of men, and most jealously guarded, were ten courts which contained fifty beautifully fitted apartments, and which were reached by a long, dark corridor. These apartments were occupied by a thousand beautiful girls, who were the king's slaves, and whom he daily visited. Beyond this seraglio was a lake, on the banks of which were pretty groves, orchards, and enclosures; and to this spot the king with his multitude of lovely damsels often repaired, sometimes driving with them in carriages, at other times on horseback. The groves were full of deer, antelopes and rabbits, and the damsels joined their master in the hunt with great zest and skill. Sometimes breakfast or dinner was spread beneath the wide spreading trees of the grove, and the king and his seraglio enjoyed their meals in the open air.

But all this had passed away when Marco was at Kinsai; for some years before Kublai Khan had besieged and taken the city, and had driven Facfur from the throne of his ancestors, and now the palace and its pleasure grounds were fast falling into decay. Instead of their king, the people were ruled over by a Tartar governor sent by the khan; and peaceably as they were disposed, they were far from contented with the dominion of a foreign despot.

Marco, however, was treated with kindness as long as he stayed, though the envoy of the khan; and at last, having accomplished his mission there, departed with his train, being followed beyond the walls by the governor and a great concourse of the people.

Continuing his journey, Marco passed through many thriving cities and pretty towns, which favorably impressed him with the value of this part of the khan's dominions, all of which had been acquired by conquest. The inhabitants were no longer Tartars, but almond-eyed Chinese; and Marco gazed upon them, with their yellow skins, their long pig-tails, their little shoes and loose dress, with much interest.

Everywhere the people seemed a most peaceful, harmless, industrious race; until Marco came to a place called Fugui, where the inhabitants were rude and ferocious, and lived apart from all the surrounding population. They were always fighting, and when they went to war, they cut their hair close to their heads, and painted their faces a deep blue, which gave them a horrible, ghastly expression. They always fought on foot, the only mounted person in the army being its chief. The prisoners they took they cooked and ate, and seemed to exceedingly relish this human food. Marco stayed in this place as short a time as possible; for his escort was not a large one, and the natives were so hostile to the rule of the khan, that he feared they might suddenly attack him.

It was time for Marco to think of returning to the khan's court, and reporting the result of his errand to the western provinces. As he reflected on all that he had seen and heard, he could not but be astounded at the wonderful civilization, riches, and activity of these far Eastern peoples, of which Europe had scarcely heard, and certainly of whose great skill in the arts and industries Europeans had not the faintest idea. He cast his eyes into the future, and foresaw the time when all these marvels would become known to the

Western world; he pictured to himself the immense trade which would grow up between the West and the East—what luxuries, comforts and adornments Europe would sooner or later derive from Asia. In his heart he was glad that he had seen all these things, and that, when he returned to Venice, he should have so thrilling a story to tell.

He took the journey back to Kambalu leisurely, pursuing much the same route as that by which he had come, and meeting with many adventures on the way. He encountered the same perils and witnessed the same wild sports, as those of his outward progress; loitered in the pleasant places, and hurried through those the memory of which was not agreeable, or the dangers of which were to be avoided.

More than a year had passed since his setting out, when, one cloudy morning, the domes and roofs of Kambalu once more met his view. He was not sorry to see them, for he should embrace his father and uncle once more, and he had news for the khan which could not fail to please his royal friend. A messenger, gone on before, had carried the tidings of his return; and when he was within a few miles of the city, he was met by his father and uncle, who had galloped out on horseback to greet him. Father and son leaped off their steeds, and were locked in each other's fond embrace. They eagerly questioned each other as to what had happened while they had parted; Nicolo remarked how stalwart, brown and sinewy Marco had grown, and how long his beard was; and Marco perceived that his father bore more wrinkles, and that his hair was more plentifully sprinkled with streaks of gray.

The khan's welcome of his faithful envoy was most cordial. He warmly embraced him, and heard his account of what he had seen and done with emphatic tokens of his pleasure. That night a noble feast was held in the great hall of the palace in honor of the wanderer's return, after which the khan ordered his jugglers and clowns to perform their most perilous and amusing feats for the entertainment of the court.

Marco now enjoyed a long period of repose from his wanderings. He found himself more firmly fixed than ever in the khan's favor, and that his position at court was more privileged and prominent than before. But having had a taste of adventure, he soon wearied of the luxurious in-dolence and ease that marked life at the palace; and when the khan proposed another expedition to him, he eagerly caught at the chance for a more stirring career.

Thus it came about that Marco often went on embassies to distant parts of the monarch's dominions. Sometimes he was accompanied by his father and uncle; sometimes they went, while he staid at home. After a time, he was oftener on his travels than idly loitering about the court. He became acquainted with all the khan's provinces, even the remotest; and was soon known and honored by all the governors and vassal kings who were subject to the khan, and even by the populations of the cities and towns.

Happily for the world, Marco had a wonderfully good memory; and he took care to make notes of the curious things he observed. So that, years after, when he was cast into prison (as we shall find), he was able to give a full narrative of all that he had seen and all that had befallen him in the romantic East.

The khan was pursuing his military operations all the time that the Polos were at his court. He was a warlike potentate, loved the din of battle, and was insatiably ambitious of adding new territory to his already vast dominions. It was rarely that a neighbor whom he had resolved to subdue could withstand him for any length of time; for so numerous and well-appointed were his armies, such was his own skill and perseverance, and such was the fierce courage of his troops that he was well nigh irresistible.

There was one large and prosperous city on the western borders of his empire, however, which defied every assault that he could make upon it. It was a valuable prize, for it was not only a good military stronghold, but also a seat of busy manufacture and highly profitable arts. To subdue this city would be to add largely to the khan's revenues; but to this advantage he was more indifferent than to the others it possessed. He would also acquire a most thrifty population, a stout defence against his enemies beyond, and a large addition to his armies. Besides, Kublai Khan was unwilling that any foreign city should rival his own in power and prosperity; he wished to rule supreme in Asia.

For three years this brave city, the name of which was Sayanfu, had held out against the imperial forces, though the khan had sent a mighty army to besiege it. The army could only approach it on one side, because on every other side the city was bounded by a wide lake. Across this lake came the provisions which enabled the garrison to hold out. The khan's troops were therefore obliged to give up the siege, and return to Cathay.

This discomfiture irritated the khan, whose will was seldom thwarted in anything he undertook and he became morose and despondent. Not long after the return of the troops, Marco Polo sought an audience of the khan; and having been admitted to his presence, as he always was freely when he asked it, addressed the downcast monarch as follows:

"Sire, I think, if you will intrust an expedition against Sayanfu to my father, my uncle and myself, we can subdue the city, and deliver it into your hands."

The khan looked up surprised, and a new hope glowed in his eyes. He had unlimited confidence in the wisdom and capacity of the Polos, and Marco's words at once aroused him from his gloom.

"And how will you do this, Venetian, when my greatest generals and bravest troops have failed?"

"We will assail the walls, sire, and batter them down. We have certain skilful men in our train. One of them, a German and a Christian, can build a powerful engine which no wall can resist; and other engines, which will hurl enormous stones to a great distance, and will thus bring the city to terms."

"Go speedily, then," cried the khan; "take such troops as you choose, and assume their command. Once more lay siege to this audacious city; and if you can take it with your engines, my gratitude will be boundless."

The Polos started forth with a numerous force. The

German and his companions were as good as Marco's word. The march was a long and dreary one; but both the Polos and the cohorts they commanded were used to hard tramping, and in a shorter time than might be believed found themselves confronting the frowning walls of Sayanfu. The machines made by the German and transported to the scene of action were soon placed in position and ere long the people of Sayanfu found their houses pelted with huge rocks, which came crashing through the roofs and spreading devastation in the streets. At the same time great battering-rams were brought near the walls, and being set in motion, made terrible breaches in them. This was a kind of warfare which the people of Sayanfu had never before seen. They soon became panic-stricken, and began to clamor to their governor and generals to give up the city. The chiefs met in council; meanwhile building after building was falling headlong, crushed by the missiles of the Tartars. At last, it was resolved to send out messengers to plead for terms of peace.

The Polos received the envoys in their camp. They told them that there was only one condition on which they would cease bombarding the city. This was, that it should submit to the dominion of the khan. There was no time to waste in parleying. The harsh terms were agreed to, and the Tartar army entered Sayanfu in triumph, and took possession of it in the name of their sovereign.

Their return to Kambalu was signalized by the wildest rejoicings. The khan was beside himself with delight, and showered honors and gifts upon the Venetians, who had so valiantly succeeded where his oldest and ablest generals had failed.

The triumph of the Polos, however, gave rise to much jealousy on the part of these generals, and other nobles of the khan's court; and it was not long before Marco heard of a plot to entice himself, his father and his uncle, out of the city to a lonely spot, and there to murder them. He divulged this plot to the khan, who instantly banished those who were concerned in it; and after that it was long before Marco heard of any further jealousy or ill will towards him and his kinsmen.

Many years had now elapsed since the arrival of the Polos in Cathay. Marco, amid all the excitements and luxury of his life there, had often sighed for home and the friends left behind, so long ago, in Venice. But when he or his father spoke to the khan of their desire to turn their steps westward towards Europe again, the swarthy potentate would not listen to such a thing. The Polos knew well that, if he had set his heart on their remaining, he could, if necessary, prevent their departure by force nor could they hope to escape secretly from his court and country. They were forced, therefore, to bide their time and await a favorable opportunity to return to Europe.

Meanwhile, Marco was destined to have many adventures, and see other peoples, as strange and interesting as those he had already visited. It was not long after their unsuccessful attempt to get away, that the khan sent him upon a longer and more interesting expedition than he had before undertaken.

CHAPTER XI.

Marco Polo in the Eastern Seas

On a hot summer morning, Marco set foot for the first time on an Oriental ship. Once more he was on his travels; and this time the greater part of his journey was to be by sea. The ship on whose deck he found himself was, to his eyes, a very curious affair; rude, when compared with European craft, yet not without its features of comfort, safety, and convenience. It was evidently constructed of fir wood, and it had but a single deck.

Marco wandered over the vessel, eager to examine its every part. He observed that the space below the deck was divided into no less than sixty cabins, very cozily fitted and furnished, most of them being used for sleeping purposes. The ship had one rudder and four masts. In the hold was a number of compartments made of very thick planks, and water-tight, so that if the vessel sprang a leak in one of them the goods might be removed to another, into which the water from the first could not penetrate. He was told that not seldom vessels were struck so hard by whales as to force in the bottom. If a leak followed the water ran on to a well, and passed out again.

The ship was very strongly built. The planks were thick, held together with stout nails, and were thickly plastered; but not with pitch, of the use of which the Tartars appeared to be quite ignorant. The vessel was propelled by oars, each of which required four sailors. In all the crew numbered two hundred men. A number of small boats, for fishing and other purposes, were hung at the sides. Marco's first destination was to the large group of flourishing islands, which lay several hundred miles off the coast of Cathay, and with which we are now familiar as Japan. It was a long and wearisome voyage, and for the first few days Marco felt all the discomforts of seasickness. After recovering from this, he began to enjoy the sea transit and gazed with much interest at the many strange-looking craft that passed and repassed within sight of his ship.

It appeared that, not many years before, the khan had attacked the Japanese islands with a large fleet and a strong army under two of his ablest generals. They landed on one of the islands, but were forced to embark from it again, on account of dangerous storms and winds that threatened the destruction of their vessels. They repaired to another island, where they sought refuge from the fury of the elements. Soon after some of their ships sailed for home, and others were destroyed by the tempests. The Japanese now descended with a large fleet upon the island to make an end of the invaders; and desembarking, advanced to attack them. The Tartars, perceiving that the enemy had left their ships, ran down to the coast and, boarding them, set sail for the largest island, leaving the Japanese in dismay and helplessness behind.

The inhabitants of the large island, seeing their own ships return, thought of course that they brought back the Japanese army. They therefore left their principal city undefended, and the Tartars entered it and held it. But soon the Japanese who had been left on the smaller island recovered their senses. They collected other ships, besieged their city, held as it was by the Tartars, and at last compelled the khan's forces to surrender. Thus the khan's expedition had failed, and the Japanese were still, when Marco made this voyage, independent of his rule. Satisfied to recover their natural liberty, the Japanese had been willing to live ever since on terms of peace and friendship with the khan and his subjects; and when Marco arrived at their islands, he found himself free to land and wander in their towns at will.

He found them a people with lighter complexions than those who dwelt on the main land, and better looking. Their pleasant manners, too, pleased him. Like the Tartars and the Chinese, they seemed very rich, and especially to have an abundance of gold. He saw a palace on the first island at which he landed which appeared to be fairly plated with gold. Even the pavements of the palace blazed with the rich metal. The Japanese also had plenty of precious stones; and among them Marco saw for the first time red pearls, which struck him as very beautiful.

Marco observed that the Japanese were idolaters, and that they worshipped idols having the heads of dogs, sheep, and pigs, and an immense number of arms and hands, spreading out from the bodies in every direction. On his asking one of them why his countrymen had such strange idols, the reply was that "our ancestors left them to us, and we shall leave them to our children."

Marco's stay in Japan was brief, for he had still a long voyage to take. His ship sailed thence southward into the sea of China, and stopped at many groups of islands, on which the young traveller landed, and where he saw many novel sights.

He was greatly struck with the number and delicious fragrance of the spice trees and shrubs that grew on these islands; and also with the abundance of gold and other precious metals which seemed to exist everywhere. At last he reached a large island called Ciampa, which was ruled over by a king who paid tribute to the khan, and who therefore welcomed Marco with such semi-barbarous hospitality as he could. The khan had some years before invaded Ciampa with a large army, and had laid waste the territory; whereupon the king had agreed to pay yearly a tribute, in the shape a number of large elephants. Every year, therefore, there arrived at the khan's court a group of these lordly beasts, which he valued more than any others he had.

Marco was amused with some of the customs of Ciampa. One was, that before any young girl on the island could be married, she must be brought before the king; and if he chose to take her for one of his wives, she must be given up to him. Thus his sable majesty had a multitude of wives, the greatest beauties in his realm; and more than a hundred sons and daughters.

After a long voyage Marco found himself among that famous group of islands that lies in a long, almost parallel line, along the southern coast of Asia. He landed on Java, which was then a powerful and independent kingdom, with a prosperous trade with India and China. The Java merchants sent their pepper, nutmegs, cloves and other rich spices to the continent, and received back grain and silks. Marco was amazed at the busy aspect of its towns and the wealth of its people. He was still more deeply interested in Sumatra, which he soon afterwards visited, and which seemed to him even richer in commerce and in natural productions. In some parts of the island he found the people very wild and barbarous; and while sojourning in one of the interior towns, he amused himself by witnessing a wild elephant hunt. The rhinoceroses there were the largest and most ferocious he had ever seen, with big black horns in the middle of their foreheads, and a most forbidding aspect. There, too, he saw the greatest multitude of monkeys of all shapes, sizes and colors, whose antics among the branches of the forest trees he watched with much glee.

Marco observed in Sumatra some mummies which, it was said, were those of a race of pigmies that dwelt in India. On examining them closely, however, he was able to detect that they were really preserved monkeys. These monkeys it appeared, were taken, skinned and shaved, and their limbs pressed so as to resemble human bodies as much as possible; and were then put in jars and sold to credulous people as dwarfs. *STOP*

4/12   Among the tribes inhabiting Sumatra, Marco found some who were cannibals; and so much afraid were the Tartars who came with him that these cannibals would catch and roast them, that they built huts of wood and twigs on the seashore, so as to defend themselves from them if attacked. In one of the tribes, if a man fell sick, his family sent for a magician and asked him if the invalid could recover. The magician, after performing incantations over him, pretended to be able to predict this. If he foretold that the man would die, the relatives made haste to strangle the sufferer, to cook his body, and invite all their friends to feast upon it. They were very careful to eat him completely up, for they believed that otherwise his soul would be in torment; and having collected the bones, they placed them in a large, beautifully ornamented coffin, which they hid away in a cavern in the mountains.

On another island, which Marco visited after leaving Sumatra, he saw some huge orangoutangs, which, it seemed, the natives believed to be hairy wild men who dwelt in the woods.

After leisurely cruising for some time among the islands in this vicinity, Marco at last came to that famous and lovely island which we know as Ceylon. The loveliness of the place was in striking contrast with the barbarous aspect and character of the natives, who, Marco noticed, went almost naked, and roamed about their picturesque mountains and forests just as if they were wild beasts. They raised no grain except rice, on which, and the flesh of the game they caught in the woods, they wholly subsisted. But savage as these people were, Marco was amazed at the number and beauty of the gems they possessed. Chief among these were the rubies, which were very large and brilliant. The king of the country had a ruby which Marco was sure was the largest in the world. Sapphires, topazes, amethysts and diamonds were also abundant.

While in Ceylon, Marco saw a lofty and jagged mountain rising from the midst of verdant hills, which it seemed impossible to ascend. Its crags rose among the clouds, and were often lost to view amid the shrouds the clouds spread about them. This, he was told, was "Adam's Peak;" and upon it was said to be the tomb of the founder of the Buddhist religion, being situated near the place where he had departed from earth. Kublai Khan had, indeed, sent thither some years before and had obtained two of the teeth, and some of the hair, supposed to belong to the god of his faith. He had also obtained a miraculous cup which had been used by this god, and which when filled with food for one man, speedily contained, it was said, enough for five.

Marco spent a long time in Ceylon, for it was the loveliest island he had yet seen in the eastern seas, and the people, though wild and almost bestial in their habits, were not quarrelsome or unfriendly. He found them, indeed, to be great cowards, who seemed afraid of the weapons which the Tartars carried in their belts; and Marco wondered why, with all their riches, they had not long since been conquered by some ambitious potentate from the mainland. He loved to wander in their beautiful groves, and to loiter under

the natural avenues of wide spreading palms; to eat of the
delicious fruit which grew there in richest profusion, and
some kinds of which were quite new to him; or to ascend
some sloping hill, and gaze out upon the sparkling sea.

It was a very short transit—only about sixty miles—from
Ceylon to the nearest point on the great peninsula of India;
and it was with deep emotion that Marco for the first time
caught sight of that famous and mighty empire. People in
Europe already knew something about India; although three
centuries were to elapse before Vasco da Gama found a
way to it by sea, around the Cape of Good Hope. Travellers
from Italy had visited its wonderful cities, and had brought
back thrilling accounts, which had reached Marco Polo's
ears in his boyhood. Of India he had learned still more at
the khan's court, for a prosperous trade existed between
India and Cathay and all that he had heard of the Hindoo
Empire made him very impatient to observe it for himself.

As he approached the coast, he saw a sight which he afterwards remembered with much interest. This was the vast
fleet of boats that were engaged in the pearl fishery. Many
large vessels were anchored in the sea for miles around,
and from these the boats with the divers went out. Marco
saw the divers, with their strange gear, plunging into the
water, and, after a few moments, drawn up again by their
comrades, holding the large shells which they had grasped
on the bottom, and in which the pearls were fixed in rows.

Marco landed on the coast of India, which at this point
was full of sand banks and coral reefs; and went into the
interior, guarded by the train of attendants whom Kublai

Khan had sent with him. Ere long he reached the chief town of the province of Maabar, where he rested from his voyage, and employed himself in observing the country and the manners and customs of the people. The king of Maabar, learning that he was from the mighty monarch of Cathay, received him with all honor, and permitted him to wander everywhere at full liberty.

The people, he perceived, went naked, except that they wore a piece of cloth about their middle. The same was true of the king himself; but to make up for want of clothes, the dusky potentate fairly glittered with rich jewelry. He wore an enormous necklace of rubies, sapphires and emeralds; and from this was suspended a long silk cord, on which very large pearls were strung. On both his arms and legs were heavy jewelled and golden bracelets.

This king had no less than five hundred wives, and freely appropriated the wives of any of his subjects when he happened to take a fancy to them; and the despoiled husbands were obliged to submit to their loss with a good grace. The king had a numerous body guard, armed to the teeth, who attended him wherever he went, and protected his palace at night. Marco was told that when a king of Maabar died, a huge funeral pyre was erected, upon which the royal corpse was placed; and that as soon as the priests set fire to it, his guards threw themselves upon it, and were burned with their master.

Marco was one day loitering in the streets of the town (which was quite a populous one) when he saw a crowd approaching, and in their midst a wagon drawn by natives.

The crowd were shouting in an excited manner; and as soon
as the wagon came near, he perceived a man standing bolt
upright in it, holding some long sharp knives. On asking
what this meant, he was told that the man had committed
some grave crime, and was being carried to the place of
execution. The crowd were calling out, "This brave man is
about to kill himself, for the love of the great idol!" Marco
followed the crowd, which stopped in an open space in the
centre of the town. Then the man in the cart began to stab
himself with the knives, first in the arms, then in the legs,
and lastly in the stomach, crying the while, "I kill myself
for love of the idol;" until, pierced by many self-inflicted
wounds, he fell expiring in the bottom of the cart. It was
supposed that thus he saved his soul.

Soon after, Marco had occasion to witness another ghastly
custom of the Hindoos, in which the wife was thrown alive
upon the burning pyre with her dead husband. The natives, besides their idols, worshipped oxen and cows, and
no power on earth could have induced them to eat beef.

Everybody in Maabar, from the king to his meanest
subject, always sat upon the ground; and when Marco asked
a Hindoo why they did not sit on chairs or benches, the
latter replied, solemnly, "We came from earth, and must
return to earth; and we cannot too much honor this common mother." Though barbarous in many of their ways,
this people were at least exceedingly neat. In this respect,
there were some European nations that might have taken
pattern from them. They never would eat until they had
washed all over; and every Hindoo took two baths each

day. They were also very temperate, rarely or never partaking of wine.

Crimes or offences against their laws were very severely punished. When a Hindoo owed another a debt and would not pay it, the creditor watched his opportunity, and drew a wide circle around the debtor with a pointed stick. If the debtor moved out of this circle without paying what he owed, he condemned himself to death. In consequence of this curious method, there were but few debtors in Maabar. Once while Marco was there, the king himself became subject to the custom. A foreign merchant, to whom the king owed a large sum, was bold enough to draw a circle around his majesty; who finding himself fairly caught by his own law, made haste to pay the debt.

After staying for some time at Maabar, Marco pursued his journey into the interior of Hindoostan, his mind full of the singular sights he had seen, and eager to observe the Hindoo races who dwelt beyond.

CHAPTER XII.

Marco Polo Among the Hindoos

NDIA, at the time that Marco visited it, was divided into a great many independent states, some Hindoo and some Mohammedan, each ruled over by its own sovereign. It was not, as now, the dependency of a great foreign power. But as India was six centuries ago, in its faith, manners and customs, and the character of its people, so it is very much to-day. Many of the manners and customs which Marco observed, still exist; and we find in the Hindoos of the present very much the same peculiar vices and virtues as those he described. Marco found the Hindoos, like most of the Orientals he had seen, very much under the influence of magicians and astrologers. They were very superstitious, and there were many omens the warnings of which they always took care to obey, believing that if they did not do so, misfortune would fall upon them. A man who set out on a journey, if he met with what he considered an evil omen, would turn back and go straight home again, no matter how near he might be to his destination, or how pressing his business. The day, hour and minute of the birth of every child were recorded, simply to enable the magicians to make predictions concerning his future life.

As soon as a boy reached his thirteenth birthday he became independent of his parents, and went out into the world to make his own living; having received a small sum of money from his father with which to make a start. They did very much as poor boys, dependent on themselves, do in our day; found something to hawk about the streets and sell, on which they could make a little profit. Near the seashore they were in the habit of watching on the beach for the pearl-boats to come in, and would buy a few small pearls of a fisherman, and carry them into the interior and sell them to the merchants. Having made a little money, they would go and buy some provisions for their mothers, who still prepared their food for them.

Marco saw many monasteries, nestling amid the mountains and hills, as he progressed through the country; and learned that these monasteries were full of idols, adorned with gold and precious stones. To the care and worship of these idols large numbers of lovely young girls were sacrificed by their parents; and these girls were in the habit, every day, of cooking very savory dishes, and placing them, with great reverence, before the hideous idols. As the idols did not descend from their pedestals and partake of the food, Marco wondered what became of it. He soon found out; for, having been admitted to one of the monasteries as a great favor, he saw the girls offer the idols their daily meal: after which they began to dance some very quick and graceful dances, singing the while a loud, wild, joyous chorus. When they ceased dancing and singing, they went up to the dishes; and, supposing the idols had eaten as much as they desired, the girls themselves devoured the contents of the plates. Marco was told that these girls remained in the monasteries until the very day of their marriage.

The priests of the monasteries at once attracted Marco's attention, so singular was their aspect, and so strange their mode of living. Many of them seemed to be very old men, with long snowy beards and bent forms; yet they had fresh, dark complexions, and were very active in their movements. Marco was told that they often lived to be a hundred and fifty or even two hundred years old; but he had now been in India long enough not to believe everything he heard. The priests lived on nothing but rice, apples and milk, and for a beverage drank a curious mixture of quicksilver and sulphur. In some of the monasteries the priests always went perfectly naked, even in winter, and slept in the open air; and led a very severe and self-denying life. The only symbol of their sacred office was a little copper or bronze ox (an animal they worshipped), which they wore on their foreheads.

These priests were always very careful not to kill any living thing; for they thought that not only animals and insects, but even fruits and flowers, had souls. They would not harm so much as a fly or a worm; and would not eat apples until they were all dried up, for they supposed them when fresh to be alive, and only dead when they were shrivelled.

When a young man sought to become a priest in the monasteries, he underwent what seemed to Marco a very amusing trial. On arriving at the monasteries, the fairest young girls belonging to it came forth to meet him; and gathering around him, overwhelmed him with kisses and embraces. The old priests, meanwhile, stood by and keenly watched him. If he betrayed any pleasure at the caresses of the girls, he was at once rejected and sent into the outer world again; but if he submitted to them coldly, and with unmoved countenance, he was admitted to the priesthood.

As the envoy of the khan, Marco was admitted into "the best society" of the places that he visited and he was much struck with the manners and virtues of the higher class of Hindoos. These comprised the class which we know as Brahmins. He could not fail to notice their high sense of honor in their dealings with each other; their truthfulness and probity; the temperance and purity of their lives. They ate no flesh and drank no wine, and as husbands were models of fidelity. The Brahmins, to designate their rank, wore a long silk thread over the shoulder, and across the breast; and so do the Brahmins of our own time. The only habit they had which Marco did not like, was that of chewing betel leaves. This made their gums very red, and was thought to be healthy; but it caused them to be constantly spitting.

Intelligent as the Brahmins seemed, they were as completely under the influence of superstition and magic as the lowest and most ignorant of their country folk. When a Brahmin merchant was about to make a bargain for some goods, he rose at sunlight, went out, and caused his shadow to be measured. If it was of a certain length, he went on with the trade. if not he postponed it to another day. This is perhaps the origin of the Eastern greeting, "May your shadow never be less!" If a Brahmin proposed to buy an animal, he went where it was, and observed whether the animal approached him from a lucky direction. If so, he bought it; but if not, he would have nothing to do with it. If, when a Brahmin issued from his house, he heard a man sneeze in a way which seemed to him of bad omen, he turned around, went into his house again, and waited till the man who had sneezed unluckily was quite out of sight. In the same way a Brahmin who, walking along a road, saw a bird approaching from the left, at once turned on his heel and went the other way. STOP

On his journey northward, Marco passed through the famous valley of Golconda, from whence came, and still come, the largest and most beautiful diamonds in the world. He found an aged queen reigning there who, though she had been a widow for forty years, was still mourning for her husband. She received Marco with a cordial welcome, and entertained him with feasts, dances and music in her palace. He delighted to wander in the picturesque valleys from which the most beautiful gems in the world were procured; to see the swift mountain torrents, as, after a storm, they swept through the declivities; and to watch the diamond-hunters who, when the freshet was over, hunted for their precious merchandise in the valleys through which the waters had passed. He was told, at Golconda, the same story about the eagles and the diamonds, that we read in Sinbad the Sailor's adventures in the "Arabian Nights;" how the people threw huge pieces of meat into the deep, inaccessible pits, to which the diamonds lying on the bottom stuck; how the eagles swooped down, caught the jewelled flesh in their talons, and on rising again were so frightened by the cries and frantic gestures of the men, that they let their precious prey drop; and how the men thus secured the diamonds which they could not otherwise reach. But Marco knew how fond the Hindoos were of telling marvellous tales; and did not give too easy a belief to what he heard.

Marco saw some of the white eagles that were said to render this great service to the diamond-hunters; but observed that most of the eagles in India were black as jet, like crows, and were much larger than those he had seen in Europe. He also saw some curious bald owls, with neither wings nor feathers; peacocks, larger than he had ever before seen; parrots of every hue and size, which he greatly admired, especially some very small red and white ones; and chickens, altogether different from European fowl.

On reaching the province of Coilon, where he found many Christians and Jews, as well as Mohammedans and Hindoos, he was deeply interested in seeing the growth of pepper, and especially of indigo, the latter being very plentiful. It was made, he observed, of an herb, which was soaked a long time in water; after which, being exposed to the hot sun, it boiled, grew solid, and thus became the indigo which everybody knows. The people of this province were very black, many shades darker than most of the Hindoos, and were less civilized than the natives Marco had hitherto seen. As he passed through the vast forests of this part of India, he espied innumerable herds of monkeys of every shape and hue, which threw down branches and nuts at him as he went along; and now and then he saw leopards, enormous wildcats, and even lions, prowling about on the edge of the woods, and in the neighboring jungles.

After travelling for many weeks in the interior of India, Marco at last reached the seashore again, and found himself on the western coast of the continent. He then went on shipboard, and passed from place to place by water, thus traversing the same coast along which, two hundred years later, Vasco da Gama sailed, and established the dominion of Portugal.

Marco soon became aware that he was in a dangerous part of the world; for the coast of Malabar was swarmed, at that time, with pirates, who had it pretty much their own way with strange vessels. Once or twice the ship in which Marco sailed was hotly pursued by these freebooters of the sea; but happily she was able to make port safely each time. Marco learned that the pirates were in the habit of signalling to each other, when a merchant vessel appeared, all along the coast, by means of brilliant lights. They were stationed five miles apart, on a line a hundred miles long; and these lights, appearing first on one corsair ship, and then on the next, telegraphed the news of a coming prize throughout this distance; so that the poor merchantman had usually but little chance of escape. The merchantmen, therefore, always went strongly manned and armed; and more than one desperate sea-fight did Marco witness on his way northward to Bombay. He was told that the pirates, on seizing a ship, took all her goods, but did not harm the crew; saying to them, "Go and get another cargo, so that we may catch you again and rid you of it."

Despite the pirates, Marco found the west coast of India fairly bustling with commerce. Every harbor seemed full of ships, and every port full of store-houses; the trade of the coast extended to Arabia and Egypt, to Africa, Australasia and Cathay. On the wharves of the seaport towns he saw the greatest variety of costumes and features, from the sober Parsee in his long flowing robe, to the heavy-turbaned Arab and the Persian with his gorgeously embroidered sack.

Even used as he was to the great warehouses of China and Cathay, he was astonished at the beautiful cloths and articles of skilful workmanship that he saw at Malabar and Bombay; the finely dressed leather, the rich embroideries, and the luxurious trappings for men, horses, and elephants; the ornaments and knicknacks of brass, gold, silver and precious gems and he was forced to confess that the bazaars of India out-rivalled those of any Oriental land he had yet visited.

Marco again set sail, and his ship now took its course across the Indian Ocean towards the coast of Africa; for his mission would not be wholly fulfilled until he had been to certain islands and kingdoms of that continent. He had already been absent from Cathay for more than a year; and found himself now quite as near his Venetian home as to the court of the great khan. There were moments, as he sped across the Indian Ocean, when he was sorely tempted to order the sailors to turn northward, to land in Egypt and make his way across that country to Alexandria, and there watch the opportunity, to take passage in a Venetian galley to the city of his birth.

But his father and uncle were far away in Cathay, and Marco could not desert them. He knew that if he did, the khan would revenge himself for such a desertion upon his kinsmen. Besides, Marco had been overwhelmed with favors, wealth and power by Kublai Khan and to prove false to his pledge that he would faithfully return, was an act of baseness of which the high-souled young Venetian was incapable.

So he kept on his course across the ocean, resolved to see all of the world that he could and, having accomplished all the objects for which he had set out, to return with his report to Cathay. On the way he stopped at two islands, called the "Male" and "Female," whose dusky inhabitants he found to be Christians; but they were very different Christians from those to whom Marco had been used in Europe. It appeared that all the men dwelt on the "Male" island, and all the women on the "Female," thirty miles away, and that the men crossed over and visited their wives and daughters once a year, remaining with them for three months and then returning to their own abode. The sons lived with their mothers until they were fourteen years of age, when they were thought to be old enough to join the community of their own sex. The two islands were ruled over, not by a king, but by a bishop; and Marco was much amused to observe that this holy potentate, instead of wearing a mitre and embroidered robes, went almost naked.

Marco landed at another island, several hundred miles south of the "Male" and "Female" islands, where the people were also Christians. They claimed to have all sorts of miraculous powers, such as the power to change the direction of the wind by their enchantments. The island was a very remote, solitary, dismal place, frequented by pirates, and Marco was very glad to get away from it after making as brief a sojourn as possible.

His next stopping place was the great island of Madagascar, off the east coast of Africa, which he found inhabited by two races. One of these was Arab, and they were men of light complexions and were well dressed; the other was Negro, as black as Erebus. Marco saw in Madagascar a large variety of animals, wild and domestic, and learned that the favorite food of the people was the flesh of camels, which he had never known to be eaten elsewhere. One species of bird he saw, enormous in size, and formidable to men and beasts, which, it was said, could lift an elephant high in the air. Marco was told that when one of these birds—they were probably what we know as condors—was hungry, he seized an elephant, and raising him in the air, let him fall to the earth, crushing him to death; and then fed upon his carcass.

Crossing to the main coast of Africa, Marco passed through the country of Zanzibar, where he saw negroes of gigantic size, quite terrible to behold, who could carry as much in their arms or on their shoulders as any four common men. They were very black and savage, and went quite naked; their mouths were huge, their teeth very regular and glistening white. The women struck Marco as singularly hideous, with their big eyes and mouths, and their coarse, clumsy shapes. He heard that this people were very warlike, and fought on the backs of elephants and camels, fifteen or twenty men being mounted on each animal; and that their weapons consisted of staves, spears, and rude swords. As they went into battle, they drank a very strong liquor, which they also gave to their elephants and camels, rendering both the beasts and their riders extremely fierce and bloodthirsty.

Marco saw in Zanzibar, for the first time in his life, an animal with which we are all now quite familiar—the giraffe; and admired exceedingly its beautiful stripes, graceful motions, and gentle actions. He also saw white sheep with black heads, and very large elephants; the latter were hunted for their tusks, which, as ivory, found its way to the remote marts of the world.

CHAPTER XIII.

MARCO POLO IN AFRICA

4/26

ROM Zanzibar, Marco ventured into a famous African country, very ancient in its history, and remarkable as the early seat of Christianity on the "dark continent." This was Abyssinia; a land which, in our own time, has attracted a great deal of attention, as the scene of a war between the English and the savage King Theodore.

In Marco's time, Abyssinia was called "Middle India," and was renowned as a great kingdom, inhabited by a bold and warlike race. He was therefore naturally very anxious to visit it, especially as he knew the Abyssinians to be Christians.

The journey thither from Zanzibar was long, difficult and dangerous. The wild, black tribes of the coast constantly menaced him and his party; and sometimes, as he proceeded up the rivers in the rude canoes furnished to him by friendly natives, he was assailed by showers of arrows and javelins, some of which did fatal work among his escort.

Nor were the menaces of the wild beasts to be despised. In the night, especially, the deep and awful stillness of the misty African jungle was roughly broken by the roaring

MARCO IN AFRICA

of hungry lions, and the bellowing of hippopotami and rhinoceroses. A constant watch was the only safety from the fell assaults of these half-famished monsters.

But Marco and his companions had now become quite used to "roughing it." His experience in the remotest parts of Tartary and China, his adventures in the islands and in the depths of Hindoostan, had not only hardened his sense of peril, but had taught him how to pass through the dangers of the jungle and the forest. In due time, the Tartar train crossed the confines of Abyssinia, and found themselves on the way to its capital.

Marco at once made himself known as an European and a Christian; and his light complexion and regular features showed the Abyssinians that he was not deceiving them, in spite of his Oriental dress and company. No sooner did they recognize him as a brother in religion, than the natives overwhelmed him with the warmth of their welcome. They entertained him on such rude fare as their huts provided; they guided him, in strong companies, through dangerous parts of the country; and they paddled him in their biggest canoes across the lakes and up the reed-bordered rivers.

The young traveller observed all that he saw and heard with the keenest interest; for he wished to carry back as minute an account as possible of this land of sable Christians. He soon learned that it was ruled over by a powerful emperor, under whom there were six kings, each of whom reigned over the six large provinces into which Abyssinia was divided. Three of these kings were Christians, and three were Mohammedans, the subjects of each being of the same faith as their sovereign. The emperor himself was a Christian. Marco also found that there were many Jews in Abyssinia, but they were not at all like the long-nosed, keen-eyed, heavily-bearded Jews whom he remembered at Venice.

Very different, too, were the Christian customs of this half-savage country from those to which he was accustomed at home. The Christians distinguished themselves from the Mohammedans and Jews, by having three marks branded on their faces; one from the forehead to the middle of the nose, and one on each cheek; and it was the branding of these marks with a red-hot iron which constituted their baptism.

It was soon evident to Marco that he was in the midst of a very warlike people. Everywhere there appeared troops of soldiers; and very often he passed large camps teeming with warriors. Nearly the whole male population seemed to be expert in the use of arms, and ready at a moment's warning to obey a summons to the battle-field. On the Abyssinian frontier were two other warlike nations, Adel and Nubia; and the emperor was almost constantly at war with one or the other.

Not many years before Marco's visit, the Abyssinian monarch had engaged in a terrific contest with the king of Adel. The cause of this war was a singular one; but it showed Marco, when he heard it related, how devoted the Abyssinians were to their religion. A Christian bishop was sent by the emperor on a pilgrimage to Christ's Sepulchre at Jerusalem. Having safely performed his errand at the

Holy City, the bishop set out on his return. His way lay through Adel. Now it happened that the king and people of that country were intense Mohammedans, and bitterly hated the Christians; so when the bishop came along, he was seized and brought before the governor of the province. The latter urged him to desert his religion, and become a follower of the prophet. But the bishop stuck firmly to his faith. Then the governor ordered that he should be taken out and circumcised. Thus cruelly outraged, the venerable prelate returned to Abyssinia, and lost no time in apprizing the emperor of what had happened.

The Abyssinian monarch was so enraged at the bishop's sad tale, that he wept and gnashed his teeth; and calling out to his courtiers, swore that the bishop should be avenged as never injured man was before. Collecting an immense army he advanced at the head of it into the heart of Adel, where he met the opposing forces of his mortal foe. The battle was long and terrific; but it ended in a sweeping victory for the invaders. The army of Adel broke and fled; and the Abyssinians, infuriated and intoxicated by their triumph, laid waste and destroyed the largest towns and fairest fields of Adel, and put many of the people to the sword. Having thus wreaked his vengeance for the bishop's wrong, the emperor returned to his own country.

Marco found in Abyssinia the greatest abundance and variety of production, and the richest and most profuse vegetation. The natives lived on rice, wild game, milk and sesame. Among the animals he saw giraffes, lions, leopards and huge apes, the largest and most intelligent he had yet encountered. The feathered creation, as it appeared in Abyssinia, struck him with wonder and admiration. The domestic fowls he thought the most beautiful in the world; the ostriches seemed "as large as asses;" and the parrots exceeded in variety of color and splendor of plumage anything he had ever imagined. He passed through many thriving towns in some of which he observed manufactories of cotton and other cloths; and by many lofty, though rudely built castles, perched on high cliffs, or on the slopes of wooded hills.

Marco would have liked to linger long in Abyssinia, which was a country that greatly attracted him on many accounts. He would have liked, also, to push on further, and explore all the wonders of Egypt and the Nile. But he had now been away from the court of the khan much longer than he had intended; and he knew that both the khan, and his father and uncle, must by this time be looking anxiously for his return.

He was forced, therefore, reluctantly, to turn his face eastward again. During his travels, he had gathered many curiosities of the strange places he had visited; and he had lost a number of the Tartars who had formed a part of his train. He had now with him only enough men to bear his baggage, and to act as a guard. Seeking a port whence to embark, he found it necessary to proceed to the great and flourishing city of Aden, the port which was the centre of all the commerce of the African and Indian seas. Arriving at Aden, Marco was surprised at its wealth and the vast amount of shipping that lay in its harbor; and at the magnificence of the sultan who ruled the city and the country round about. He had no difficulty, in so busy a place, in chartering a vessel to take him and his company back to Tartary; and ere many days once more found himself on the great deep, full on the way to Kambalu. STOP

4/12 The voyage was a long, tedious, and stormy one. Sometimes Marco despaired of ever seeing the land again, so furious were the cyclones and tempests of wind and rain; sometimes they were becalmed for days and weeks. Marco landed at many of the islands he had visited on his outward voyage, and saw some which he had before passed by; but he did not, throughout the long transit, often touch at points on the mainland.

At last, however, the long voyage was over. The coast of Cathay appeared in a long, dim line at the horizon; then familiar cities and towns came into view; finally, the good ship neared the port whence Marco had set out; and it was with a full heart that he jumped upon the shore, and knew that ere long he would be clasped in his father's arms, and receive the welcome and the praises of the great khan.

His return to Kambalu was celebrated by rejoicings in which the whole court took part; for the Tartar nobles had never known of so great and indefatigable a traveller as Marco had proved himself to be. His exploits, the dangers by sea, savages and beasts through which he had passed, the wonderful countries and curious customs he had witnessed, and the valuable services he had rendered to the khan, made him a real hero, even among generals who had fought great battles, and nobles who wielded powers inferior only to those of Kublai Khan himself.

Nicolo was proud of his son's achievements, and was never done praising him. The khan grew fonder than ever of Marco, and lavished the costliest gifts and the rarest favors upon him. He made him a noble of his empire; he called him almost daily to sup with him; he offerred to marry him to one of the most beautiful, rich and high-born maidens of his realm; he gave him a stable full of beautiful horses; and consulted him upon the most important affairs of state.

By and by the warmth of the khan's affection for Marco began to fill the proud and fierce breasts of the Tartar barons with jealousy; and now Marco had to feel the bitterness as well as the sweets of good fortune. He was constantly threatened with snares and assassination. He was forced to go armed, and protected by a strong guard, lest a secret attack should be made upon him. So his life at the court, surrounded as it was with every luxury and privilege that heart could wish, became anything but a comfortable one.

Nicolo and Maffeo Polo, as well as Marco, aroused the hostility of many of the barons; and so unpleasant did their position at the court begin to be, despite the fondness and favor of the monarch, that they often talked together anxiously about the prospect of their being able to return to Venice.

Sixteen years had elapsed since the day on which they had bidden farewell to their native city. The two elder Polos were growing old; their hair was gray, their faces were wrinkled, and their strength was waning. Marco himself, who had departed from Venice a stripling, was now a stalwart, broad-shouldered man, between thirty and forty, with a heavy brown beard and the strength of a lion. Their mission in Cathay had been accomplished; for they had persuaded the khan to be a Christian, had converted many of his subjects, and had acquired great wealth for themselves.

They finally resolved to make a vigorous attempt to persuade Kublai Khan to allow them to depart, and to provide them with the means of doing so safely. The first day, they said to each other, that Kublai seemed in a particularly good and indulgent humor, they would proffer their petition.

Not long after this, the khan gave a great feast; and afterwards witnessed, with his court, the exciting sports with which he was wont to beguile the pleasant afternoon hours, after he had eaten and drunk his fill.

Retiring, then, to the shade of his park, Kublai Khan reclined under the trees, and called about him his favorite courtiers and wives. Near him were the three Polos, who observed that the monarch was in high spirits. He jested pleasantly with his companions, and lolled luxuriously on his cushions.

The Polos gave each other significant glances; and at a favorable moment, Nicolo advanced and prostrated himself at the monarch's feet.

"I have an immense favor to ask of your majesty," he said, clasping his hands, and raising his eyes to Kublai's face, "and implore you to listen kindly to it."

"And what favor can you ask, good Venetian, that I will

not grant? You and your brother, and your brave, stout son, have served me nobly these many years; how can I refuse what you ask?"

"But I fear to offend your majesty, by asking for more than you are willing to give. We beg for no more riches, no more honors. These your majesty has lavished upon us far beyond our deserts. You have loaded us with your favors and your gold. It is, indeed, many, many years that we have lived in the sunshine of your royal countenance; so many, that my brother and I have waxed old in your service. And after this long time, sire, our hearts yearn for our native land, for those beloved ones of whom we have not heard a word; and we would fain return, to tell Europe of the wonders of your vast realm, and the lofty virtues that dwell in your royal breast. Pray, your majesty, give us permission to go back to Venice; that is the petition we would lay at your feet.

The khan at first frowned, and impatiently shook his head; then smiled, and said:

"Venetian, I cannot let you go. You are too useful to me. Whom could I send as an envoy to my remote provinces, if Marco were not here? Who could teach my people how to be Christians, if you departed? No, no, stay in content, Venetians; and whatever your present possessions may be, they shall be doubled from my treasure-house. Whatever you desire to make you rich, to give you pastime, to afford you ease and content in Cathay, shall be yours. Choose your dwelling, your horses, your servants, your guards, and they shall be granted to you. But think not of going hence; it cannot be,"

Nicolo continued to plead with all the eloquence he could command; but his prayers were quite in vain. The khan was good-naturedly deaf to his entreaties. He then tried another way of gaining his object.

"Sire," said Nicolo, "Our good fortune here, and your bounteous favor, have made us bitter enemies among your barons and courtiers. They are jealous to see the affection of their monarch bestowed upon foreigners; and they hate to perceive all your most secret trusts and counsels confided to us, who are of strange birth and blood. Should we depart, these nobles would no longer entertain feelings so angry, and would once more gather, a united band, about your throne. For the sake, then, of peace in your court and palace, grant our prayer."

The khan looked around among his courtiers with lowering and threatening brow.

"Who dares," he cried, "to murmur at my sovereign will; who would forbid my choice of such counsellors as I please to have? Point out, Venetian, the men of whom you speak!"

"Sire, I see none among those who are present; nor do I wish to breed further discontent and quarrels in your palace, by naming those who are jealous of us. But I assure you, there are such; nor will they ever be at rest until we have forever set our faces towards the west."

The khan, however, was obdurate; and although the Polos again and again besought him to let them go, he would not budge an inch from his resolution to keep them with him. There seemed to be no help for them. The Polos could not hope to escape by stealth from Cathay; for every highroad was guarded by faithful troops of the khan, and his couriers, with their relays of horses, could travel much more swiftly than they could hope to do.

They once more reluctantly gave up the hope of returning home, and began to say to each other that, in all probability, they were destined never to set eyes on Venice more, but to live and die in Cathay. Marco resumed his idle life at court, finding a relief from its pleasures in writing out an account of his travels. In the early summer, he went in the khan's innumerable train to the imperial hunting grounds in the north; and as he had now become one of the most stalwart and skilful huntsmen of the court, he plunged with new ardor into the lusty sports of the forest and the jungle.

Marco little thought as, the summer over, he was returning again, in the wake of the imperial caravanserai, to Kambalu, that events had happened in his absence which would hasten the return of himself, his father and his uncle to Venice; and on arriving at the palace, was overjoyed to find that good fortune had suddenly opened a way for their final departure.

CHAPTER XIV.

Homeward Bound

WHILE the khan had been away with his court at the hunting grounds, three Persian ambassadors, with a gorgeous train, had arrived at Kambalu. Finding the khan away, they resolved to await his return, and were therefore sumptuously lodged in his palace. No sooner had the khan heard of their arrival, than he gave a splendid banquet in their honor; and, having feasted on the bounteous good things that his stewards set before them, the ambassadors were summoned into the garden, where the khan reclined in the midst of his women, to inform him of the object of their visit. The three Polos, as usual, had their places near the monarch. They watched with no little interest the appearance of the Persians, and listened intently to what they had to say.

The chief ambassador, making low salaams, advanced to Kublai Khan, and kneeling at his feet, spoke:

"Your majesty knows that our great sovereign, King Argon of Persia, married a lady of Cathay for his wife. With much grief I have to announce that the good Queen Bolgana is no more. She was a most gracious queen, beloved of all her lord's subjects; and the king himself loved her

157

most faithfully. When she died, with her last words she implored King Argon on no account to take to himself a Persian as his second wife, but to send hither for a maiden of her own family, and make this maiden her successor. King Argon paid heed to the dying prayer of the queen; and hath, in compliance with it, sent us here to Cathay, to seek for a second wife."

"You are very welcome, noble Persians," replied Kublai Khan, "and I shall give orders that you be entertained at my court, as long as you choose to tarry, in a manner befitting your rank and my love for King Argon, your master. You and your gallant company shall be lodged within my palace, and all things in it shall be at your service. Meanwhile, I will send messengers without delay to the province whence Queen Argon came, and will demand of her family a maiden who shall return with you to Persia."

The Persians then retired, and the khan and his courtiers resumed their recreations. The Polos soon made the acquaintance of these envoys of King Argon. Nicolo and Maffeo had twice travelled in Persia, and had already been received at the sovereign's court, and they well understood the native language of the envoys; while the latter were delighted to find accomplished Europeans, with whom they could freely talk, and who were familiar with their own country. Marco busied himself with providing amusements for the Persians, and acted as their guide about the palace park and the city of Kambalu. Occasionally he went with them on hunting parties; and soon became very intimate and confidential with them. He did not conceal from his new friends how long and eagerly he and his father had desired to return to Venice, and how resolutely Kublai Khan had forbidden them to think of doing so. The Persians sympathized with him in his longing, and encouraged him to hope that his deliverance might not be far off. But Marco drew little comfort from their words, and did not once suspect that they would themselves be the means of opening the way to his return home. Kublai Khan was as good as his word to the Persian envoys. He lost no time in sending to the native province of Queen Bolgana to demand a new bride for the Persian monarch, giving orders that the youngest and fairest daughter of the family should be sent. In due time his messengers returned, and with them the newly destined bride.

Marco was at the court when she entered the palace, and was brought into the presence of the khan and of the Persian ambassadors; and, accustomed as he was to the beauty of many of the Tartar ladies, he was amazed at the exceeding loveliness of this young girl, whose fate it was to be sent to a far-off strange land, and to become the wife of a king more than double her own age. She was very young and girlish, being scarcely seventeen; her graceful and slender form was attired in robes of the richest silk. The khan presented her to the Persian envoys, who did not conceal their admiration of her beauty, and declared that she could not fail to greatly please their lord and master.

Preparations were now hastened for the departure of the embassy. Kublai Khan had resolved that the bride should be attended with great state on her journey to her new home. He provided a brilliant escort of courtiers and guards, and selected some of the choicest gems and gold and silver ornaments that his treasure-houses provided, as presents for King Argon and his youthful bride. Upon the latter he showered necklaces, bracelets, and rings enough to dazzle even a queen; and he also gave the ambassadors solid proofs of his esteem.

The time had nearly arrived for their departure, when, one day, the chief of the ambassadors sought an audience of the khan, and told him that he was about to ask a still greater favor than the khan had as yet conferred upon him.

"At your majesty's court," said the Persian, "are three noble and learned Venetians, who have been here, as I learn, some seventeen years. Sire, they are most anxious to return to their own land. They have served you faithfully and they seek the reward of their fidelity in your gracious permission that they shall again behold the scenes of their youth. These Venetians have much knowledge of the Indian seas, by which we are about to return to Persia; and we are bold enough to beg your majesty's leave to take them with us."

Kublai Khan frowned, and at first seemed on the point of breaking out in a fit of passion; but governing his temper, turned abruptly around, and said that he would think of the Persian's request and give him his answer on the morrow. The next day he called the Persian to him and said:

"The Venetians have attached themselves strongly to me, and have been, for many years, my wisest and most trusted counsellors. I am most loth to part with them. But

I clearly see that they are fully resolved to go back to Venice, and that they cannot possibly reconcile themselves to remaining in Cathay. I perceive that they have begged you Persians to intercede for them; nor, methinks, will they leave any stone unturned to break away from me. I have therefore resolved, at last, to grant your request, and to set them free to go back with you, if so it pleases them."

The Persian bent low before the khan, in abject token of his gratitude; and then hastened off to impart his good news to Marco, who could scarcely believe that the obdurate khan had really yielded. He soon, however, received from the khan's own lips the assurance of the truth; and his heart thrilled with joy to think that, after all, he would see dear old Venice once more.

So it was decided that the Polos should go with the party of the young bride to Persia, and make their way from thence, as they could, to Europe. They soon made ready for the voyage (for the party were to travel by sea, the land journey being too long and too perilous for the frail young princess and her female companions); and the day quickly came for them to bid adieu to the good khan who had treated them so generously, and to the host of Tartar friends whom they were about to leave forever.

The khan had not only loaded down the Polos, the envoys and the princess with costly gifts, and provided them with a brilliant Tartar escort, but had caused thirteen of his largest and finest four-masted ships to be especially fitted up for their use, and to be manned by ample crews of from one to two hundred sailors each. Everything on

these ships was arranged for the luxury of the traveller.
The furniture was elegant and comfortable, and the stock
of provisions was choice and abundant. In all, the company
that attended the party comprised, besides the sailors, six
hundred persons. *STOP*

5|3   Just before they set out, Kublai Khan summoned the
Polos before him, in the presence of the whole court; and
tenderly embracing each of them, with tears in his eyes,
he handed Nicolo two golden tablets, which were to serve
them as passports. On these tablets the khan had caused to
be written his command to all his governors and subjects,
not only to permit the Polos a safe passage, but to provide
them with all things of which they might be in need.

When the travellers repaired to the port where lay their
ships, Kublai Khan, with a great multitude of courtiers and
soldiers, proceeded with them some miles on the road, and
parted from them with the warmest demonstrations of affection at a village where all halted for the leave-taking. The
khan fairly wept as he embraced Marco, who was his chief
favorite; while Marco himself was overcome with emotion
at separating from a monarch who had overwhelmed him
with favor and kindness.

The ambassadors, the princess and the Polos, having
arrived at the port of embarkation, repaired on board the
flag-ship, in which they were all to sail together; their escort and attendants entered the other ships; and, while an
enormous multitude roared its good-bye from the shore,
the fleet set forth on its southward voyage.

Marco had already traversed these Eastern seas, and

was quite familiar with the various islands and headlands as they were passed. He took command of the fleet, and under his directions the ships sailed by the nearest route into the Australian waters. They did not deem it wise or necessary to put in at any of the islands, as they had already on board provisions and water enough to last them two years, and it was needless to risk an attack from the savage inhabitants.

It took the fleet fully three months to reach the long and lovely island of Sumatra. On the voyage, Marco greatly enjoyed the companionship of the three Persians, who were men of high birth and remarkable intelligence. On making the acquaintance of the young princess, (whose name was Cocachin), he found her as lively and amiable as she was lovely in face and person. She was soon able to converse with her protectors, and spent much of her time on deck, gazing amazed at the myriad wonders of the sea, which she had never before beheld. At first she had been homesick, and melancholy; but the excitements of the voyage had restored the rosy color to her cheeks, and gayety to her heart.

After staying a short while at Sumatra, the ships resumed their voyage, their stores replenished, and their company refreshed by the brief sojourn on land. Sailing southwestward, they skirted the coast of India as far as Ceylon; and then, turning their prows northwestward, traversed the Indian ocean, thus in due time reaching the Persian Gulf. By the time they reached the port of Hormuz, however, they had been more than two years away from Kambalu, during which period they had only landed once, at Sumatra. Two of the Persian envoys had died on the voyage.

The brilliant company landed on Persian soil with great pomp and display, for they were escorting the future queen of the country, and the envoy who survived deemed that she should make her first appearance among her future subjects in all proper state. But no sooner had they landed than they learned that the good King Argon had in their absence followed his first queen to the grave. The country was in a state of civil war, and the young Princess Cocachin had arrived to find herself widowed before she was a wife.

The party lost no time in repairing to the prince who was then ruling in Southern Persia, Kiacatu, the brother of Argon; to whom they presented their lovely charge. But Kiacatu, though engaged in a struggle with King Argon's son, Casan, for the crown, was too honorable to detain the young girl; and directed her escort to proceed with her to Casan's camp in the north, providing the party with two hundred horsemen to protect them.

Marco now found himself traversing the same road as that by which he had travelled to Cathay. Many objects were familiar to him as he advanced; and now and then, on stopping at a town or village, he found old men who remembered his journey more than twenty years before.

It was a long jaunt from Hormuz to Khorassan, where the young King Casan was posted with his army; and their progress was often interrupted by the operations of war. But everywhere the soldiers and the people respected the cavalcade, on account of the fair young princess whom they were conducting to the northern camp. Marco always rode at her side, with the ambassador; and had she not been of rank so much above his own, and the destined bride of another, he might easily have fallen head over ears in love with her. As it was, she became very much attached to her handsome and sturdy cavalier; and looked forward with real sorrow to parting from him.

It was towards evening that the company approached the camp of the gallant young prince who was fighting for the crown which was his due. The tents were spread over a wide space in a beautiful valley, watered by a swiftly-flowing stream; and from a hill top Marco surveyed the bustling scene. The soldiers were loitering about their tents in groups; and above the tents floated the banners of the royal house of Persia. In their centre was a lofty and handsome pavilion; and this the travellers rightly guessed to be the headquarters of the prince himself.

With the passports they had, it was no difficult matter to penetrate the outposts, and advance to the royal pavilion. On reaching it, the princess, ambassador, and three Polos dismounted and approached the door. Presently Prince Casan, apprized of the arrival of the party, emerged from the pavilion. He was a fine looking young man, tall and straight, with broad shoulders, a fresh rosy complexion, and a soft brown beard. He was splendidly dressed in silk and jewels, and altogether presented a noble and attractive appearance. He stepped forward and welcomed the party to his camp. Then the ambassador, standing with bowed head, informed Casan that this was the young princess of Cathay, whom his father Argon had sent for, in order to make her his wife. But now that Argon was dead, he knew nothing else to do with her, than to bring her to Argon's son and heir, Casan himself. The prince was already glancing with tender eyes at the lovely young maiden; and no sooner had the ambassador done speaking than he exclaimed: "You have done well, my lord. The fair princess shall receive all honor and protection from me. Nay, I am happily still unmarried; and the bride whom my august father destined as his queen, I will receive as mine."

So saying, he took the blushing Cocachin by the hand and led her to a tent near by, sending her women after her to keep her company. It may well be believed that she did not much regret, after all, finding that her destined spouse was no more; for he was an old man, and now she was to be married to one as young, handsome, and powerful as the proudest princess could wish.

Meanwhile, Casan busied himself with offering such hospitalities as his camp afforded to his visitors. The ambassador and the Polos were provided with luxurious tents, and at night were feasted by the prince to their hearts' content; and the next day a great review of the troops was held, at which they rode beside the prince himself.

Eager as Marco was to see Venice once more, it was with much reluctance and sorrow that he parted from the good friends with whom he had travelled so far, and whose friendship he had so keenly enjoyed. The Polos resolved to tarry at the camp at least until Casan and Cocachin were married, after which event they would hasten towards home. The more Casan saw of the young girl, the fonder he grew of her; and he soon became impatient to be wedded to her as soon as possible. Cocachin was nothing loth; and so within a week of her arrival in the camp, they were duly married according to the rites of the faith to which they belonged.

The next day, the Polos prepared to set out for Trebizond, which was the nearest port where they could hope to find a ship to take them to Constantinople, from whence their way home would be easy. When the moment for bidding farewell came, Marco could not restrain his tears. He warmly embraced his Persian friends, and kneeling at the feet of the Princess Cocachin, fervidly kissed her hand. She, also, was much touched at parting from so good and faithful a friend, and tears of regret coursed down her cheeks.

The Polos here bade good-bye also to the larger part of the escort who had accompanied them on their travels, and only took with them a few guides and attendants, and a body of Persian cavalry, whom Prince Casan detailed to guard them as far as Trebizond. They then set out, followed by the friendly cries of the Persian soldiers.

CHAPTER XV.

A Strange Welcome

ARCO and his party reached Trebizond in safety, having crossed the Armenian mountains, and seen with great interest still another phase of Oriental life. Trebizond was then a very thriving port of the Black Sea, and Marco was delighted when his eyes greeted, among the crowded shipping in the harbor, several vessels from which floated the once so familiar Venetian flag. There were also Cossack, Circassian, Greek and Moorish vessels, each with its peculiar and striking characteristics.

It was not long before an opportunity occurred of procuring a passage across the Black Sea to Constantinople; and the weary travellers, worn and bronzed by long wanderings, at last found themselves snugly ensconced in a European cabin. The passage across the Black Sea was a rapid and pleasant one. Soft winds blew, and the sky remained serene throughout the voyage. Yet it seemed a long voyage to Marco, who, now that he once more found himself among Europeans, was doubly eager to reach home.

One morning he awoke to find the vessel entering the narrow strait of the Bosphorus, its high banks on either side crowned with fortresses, and with the stately residences of the Greek nobles who chose to live near the metropolis of the empire. A brief sail brought them within sight of the domes and minarets of Constantinople itself; and soon Marco once more put foot upon dry land, and was threading the narrow winding streets of the famous city.

The stay of the Polos at Constantinople was not a long one. Nicolo had some business to transact with Levantine merchants, whose large warehouses stood upon the quay, and who only recognized their old acquaintance with difficulty, so entirely had he changed during his twenty years' residence at Cathay. Happily, there were Venetian galleys in port; and on one of these, bound for home, the party was able to procure a passage. Setting sail once more, they swiftly sped through the picturesque Sea of Marmora and then entered the channel of the Hellespont, of which Marco had read much in his ancient histories. From the Hellespont they issued into the Aegean Sea, and were now full on the way to Venice. The galley stopped at several Greek ports on the way; and Marco had an opportunity which he eagerly seized, to observe the monuments and traits of that noble race, which had now reached its period of rapid decline.

Ere many days had passed, Marco found himself sailing up the Adriatic, and so vivid had been his first impressions of his outward voyage, that at twenty years' distance he easily recognized many of the objects he espied along the shores. The weather continued propitious from the time they left Constantinople; it seemed as if the elements were giving the travellers a smiling and sunny welcome back to

Europe again.

It was late in the afternoon of a mellow autumn day, that, far off in the northern haze, Marco saw dimly rising from the waters the well-known domes and palaces of his beloved Venice. He could with difficulty contain himself for joy. He could scarcely speak, so deep were his emotions at beholding the longed-for sight. The three travellers stood on the deck of the galley, and, shading their eyes from the sun's rays with their hands, strained their eyes towards their native city.

Nearer and nearer they approached it; each object became every moment more distinct. The big dome of St. Mark's, the column of the lion, the spires of many churches, the broad, ornate facade of the doge's palace, came, one by one, into view; and now gondolas began to appear, gliding swiftly and noiselessly in every direction across the glassy bay. Then the mouth of the Grand Canal, flanked on either side by its palaces and churches, was easily recognized; and, before the Polos had done pointing out to each other, with eager delight, the familiar points, they found the galley drawing up to the quay. It was soon moored, and the Polos tremblingly prepared to disembark.

What had become of all their relatives and friends, whom they had left behind so many years before? It could not be but they would find many of them dead, and it was certain that all would have, like themselves, greatly changed. To land once more at Venice, therefore, after such an absence, was to encounter pain, and to exist for a time in feverish suspense.

The galley in which they had come was to remain at Venice for some time; and the three travellers left such baggage as they had brought with them from the east on board of her, while they landed and visited home once more. It happened that all three of the Polos wore the rough travelling costumes which they brought from Cathay. Their clothes were not only rough and shabby, but were of Tartar make; so that they looked much more like Tartars than Venetians. The two elders wore long pointed caps of fur, and coats that fell to the ground. About their waists were belts, from which hung yataghans and scimitars such as those used by Tartar soldiers. Marco had a flat fur cap, with a long tassel; very much such a head-gear as some Chinese mandarins wear at the present day. Maffeo Polo led with him, by a stout chain, a great shaggy dog that he had brought with him from Tartary. All three, moreover, were very dark, their skins having been tanned almost to the color of their Tartar friends, by long residence in a tropical clime, and long journeyings through rude and difficult lands. They wore long, shaggy, beards, those of Maffeo and Nicolo being quite gray; and their hair fell in tangled mats down over their shoulders. On their feet were the short, thick shoes, turned up at the ends, which every one wore in Cathay.

They thus presented, as they tramped across the square of Saint Mark, a very strange and striking appearance to the good folk of Venice whom they met; and many turned around and stared after them with no little astonishment. Not far from the square, they took a gondola, and, as well as

they could, directed the gondolier to row them to Nicolo's
house. They found that, in so long an absence, they had
actually almost forgotten their native tongue. It was as
much as they could do to make the gondolier understand
them; they had to stop, and scratch their heads, and search
their memories, for the simplest word; for they had got
accustomed at the khan's court, to talk with each other, as
well as with the Tartars, in the Tartar language, and had
long ceased to speak Italian altogether.

The street of San Giovanni Chrysostomo, on which stood
the home of the Polos, was not far distant from the Square
of St. Mark; and the swift gondola soon brought them to
the broad flight of steps which led up to it. Marco felt a
curious emotion at finding himself once more speeding
across the canals in one of the boats familiar to his youth;
while Nicolo and Maffeo could not but call to mind their
former return from Cathay.

Everything in the street where their home stood looked
much as they remembered it. Neither fire nor improvements
had done away with any of the neighboring buildings. There
were the same stairways, the same ornamental portals, the
same snug balconies, the same pretty cupolas, the same air
of indolent quiet and repose, which they so well remembered. There, too, stood the old home, as stately and silent
as of old, with the dainty carving around the arch of the
door, the same handsome cross set in the wall just above
it, and the same coat-of-arms, with its bars and initials, on
the wall at the side. It looked just as if everything had gone
on as usual for twenty years; as if it were but the other day

that the travellers had set out from that spot, followed by the tearful farewells of their families and friends.

No sooner had they landed and advanced toward the door, than a group of curious neighbors, mostly women and children, gathered closely around them, staring at them with all their might. Such strange, uncouth figures, surely, they had never seen; nor could those good people imagine what the foreign looking men were doing at the door of the big Polo house. STOP

Marco knocked loudly upon the portal. At first, no response came to his summons; but presently several women leaned out of the windows above, glared at the strangers, and somewhat curtly demanded what they wanted. They were evidently taken for foreign vagabonds and tramps; their rough, shabby coats, and bronzed and bearded faces, confirmed this idea. Nor were the suspicions of the women at the windows diminished when Marco tried in vain—so hard did he find it to speak his native tongue—to explain who they were, and what they were there for.

At last, however, the people consented to open the door, and admit the three men into the courtyard, where the entire household gathered around them. Marco addressed himself to the butler, a stout, pompous person, who had entered the family service long after the departure of the travellers; and at last made him understand that they were really Nicolo, Maffeo, and Marco Polo. The butler stared at him as if he did not believe a word he said; and then called two old women who were in the group to come forth and see if they could recognize the strangers. The old dames placed their hands on their hips, stooped down, and narrowly scanned the countenances of all three.

"Pooh, pooh," exclaimed one of them, in a shrill voice, "We know you not. You are a set of impostors."

"Besides," added the other, "Messer Nicolo and Messer Marco are dead long ago. It is years since we heard that they were killed by a band of robbers, away off there in the East."

By this time a crowd of neighbors had penetrated the court-yard, and were gathered in a close group about the travellers. Among them were several old men and women, who had seen the Polos before they went to Cathay. To these the butler appealed but one and all shook their heads. Stare as hard as they might, no one could recognize their old acquaintances in these rugged features.

"But where is Messer Marco the elder?" Nicolo asked, anxiously, in broken Italian, looking about him. "And young Maffeo, the son of Nicolo?"

"Messer Maffeo," responded the butler, pompously, "is away in the country, on a hunt. Messer Marco is dead long ago."

"Alas, poor Marco!" exclaimed Nicolo, with a deep sigh. Then, turning to the group, he added, "Very well, good friends, since you deny me in my own house, and my son is at a distance, we will repair to an inn, and await an opportunity to prove to all that we are the persons we represent ourselves to be."

With this Nicolo walked out of the courtyard of his own house, followed by Maffeo and Marco, and all three betook themselves to an inn not far distant.

The rumor of the arrival of the three strangers was soon spread through the neighborhood and the city; and a large number of their old friends and acquaintances came to see them at the inn. But, though there were some who thought they saw a dim likeness in the strangers' faces to the old friends they asserted themselves to be, nearly all denied that they perceived the least likeness whatever. Besides, the fact that the Polos were so shabby, and looked and appeared so destitute, gave a general impression that they were impudent pretenders, who were trying, by this device, to obtain the Polo property.

The affair was getting to be serious; for some time must elapse before young Maffeo and other relatives at a distance could be apprized of their arrival, and return to recognize and welcome them.

At last Nicolo hit upon a plan by which he thought they would be able to prove their identity, and win the recognition of all; and without delay the three set about putting the plan into execution.

They sent forth and invited all the old friends and acquaintances whom they could find to be living, and in Venice, to meet them at a grand banquet at Nicolo's house on a certain evening; and so earnest were they in asserting their ability to prove themselves what they claimed, that those left in charge of the house reluctantly consented that the banquet should be held there. They did not believe there would be any banquet at all, and suspected that before the appointed time, the strange men would slip away from the city, and be well rid of.

The night of the banquet, warm and serene, came; and about an hour before the guests were expected to arrive, the three Polos came to the house accompanied by porters bearing large boxes, and asked to have an apartment set aside for them, where they might make their toilet for the festivity. This request was grudgingly granted to them, and they entered the room where their boxes had been deposited and locked themselves in.

The banquet was prepared with great splendor and expense and in due time the invited friends began to flock in, and gazed with astonishment at the bounteous feast that was spread in the great hall. They assembled in a large apartment just beyond, and there awaited the entrance of their singular hosts.

They had not long to wait; for in a few moments the doors of the apartment were thrown open, and the three men entered. As soon as they appeared, there was a general exclamation of surprise and admiration. No longer attired in the uncouth costume of Tartars, no longer shaggy of hair and ragged of aspect, the three Polos presented themselves in gorgeous robes of crimson satin, that reached to the floor. Their hair and beards had been cut to the prevailing fashion in Venice; and on their necks and fingers sparkled jewels of dazzling brightness and enormous size.

The guests gathered around them, and some cried out at once that they recognized the strangers as the three Polos who had been supposed to be long ago dead. Others hung back, and still suspected that the company were being made the victims of a trick.

With graceful courtesy, however, the Polos conducted their guests to the groaning tables, and the feasting began. They talked to those who sat next to them in a free, easy strain, and with a manner as if they were the undoubted lords of the house. After the first course, the three Polos rose from the table, and, while the company moistened their hands—a custom practised in Venice after each course— retired to their apartment.

By the time the second course was served, they had reappeared, this time in fresh and still more brilliant costumes of crimson damask, with new bracelets and rings on their necks and fingers. Behind them came attendants, bearing the satin robes they had just taken off; and these they ordered to be cut up on the spot, and divided among the servants. They then resumed their seats, and once more made merry with their guests.

In due time all the courses had been served, and the company had grown gay and boisterous with the meat and wine. The cloth was removed and the servants were ordered to leave the banqueting room; and then Marco rose, and turning to the guests, said,

"My friends, you have doubted that we are the Polos, and have denied us with much scorn and scoffing. You did this because, when we arrived from our long journey, our hair and beards were long and straggling, our faces scarred and sunburnt; and also because, ragged and miserable as we looked, you took us to be poor, scheming beggars. Now you see us trim and kempt, and some of you recognize in our faces, thus restored, something of the Polo look. It still remains to prove to you that we are not beggars, forced by want to make false pretensions to a name that is not ours."

So saying, he strode through the room, and for a moment disappeared. He soon returned, bringing on his arm the shabby Tartar coats in which they had made their appearance in Venice.

Laying them upon the table, while the guests gathered curiously around him, Marco began to rip open the seams of the rough coats. Presently out from between the seams rolled a great number of large and beautiful diamonds and emeralds, pearls, torquoises, rubies and sapphires! Seam after seam was torn open, and more and more jewels fell upon the table; until there was a pile of them equal in value to a very considerable fortune.

"You see, my good friends," said Marco, "that we have not returned from Cathay quite penniless. Before leaving the court of the great khan, we turned all our property into these jewels, which might be easily carried; and in order both to carry and to conceal them safely, we had them sewed up as you see, in these rude garments."

The company could no longer doubt that the three men before them were really the long-absent Polos; and one and all crowded around them, eager to be forgiven for having at first denied them.

Ere many days had passed, young Maffeo, hearing of the return of his relatives, reached home, and was locked in the embrace of his father and brother; and now the wanderers heard the news of all that had happened during their absence of nearly a quarter of a century. The elder Maffeo's wife had also died, and this intelligence for a while filled him with grief: but happily his children still lived, though they had grown up, and were scattered in different parts of Italy.

The Polos were soon cozily settled once more in their old home and enjoyed, it may well be believed, the rest and luxury which it afforded after their weary travels.

CHAPTER XVI.

Marco Polo Goes to the Wars

T the time of his return to Venice, Marco Polo was forty-one years of age, and in the full vigor and prime of life. His wanderings and rough career had given him a powerful frame, and great bodily strength, and had implanted in him a taste for adventure and action which ill-suited him for the tranquillity of city and commercial life.

No sooner had his identity been fully recognized, than all Venice hastened to do him, as well as his father and uncle, all honor. Every day their house was thronged by nobles and great ladies, by hosts of old friends and new, anxious to pay their homage to the heroic travellers. An office of high rank was conferred on the elder Maffeo; Nicolo became one of the chief gentlemen of the doge's court; and Marco was overwhelmed with favors, honors and attentions by the ruler of Venice. Fetes were given in celebration of their happy return; and it was with difficulty that they could escape the profuse attentions which were showered upon them.

Marco became a special hero and favorite with the young Venetians who vied with each other in seeking his

friendship and companionship. Scarcely a day passed that
Marco did not receive, at his father's house, a company
of young men, who sat eagerly listening to the wonderful
stories he had to tell them of the East. They plied him with
a multitude of questions about Cathay and the great khan,
and he pleased them all by the willingness and pleasant
manner with which he replied to every one.

It happened that Marco, in describing the magnificence
of Kublai Khan's palace and court, unconsciously gave the
name to his house by which it was long after known. He
constantly repeated the word "millions" in speaking of the
khan's treasure and possessions. The khan had, he said,
millions of money, millions of subjects, millions of jewels,
and so on; so that the young men laughingly called him
"Messer Marco Millions;" and from this the Polo house
became known as the "Court of the Millions."

When the excitement and rejoicings attending their
return home were over, Marco looked about him to see
what he could do with himself. After such a life as his had
been, he did not look forward with pleasure to a career of
mere indolence. Amply rich by reason of the treasures he
had brought with him from Cathay, he was not compelled
to contemplate entering into business. He desired some
active, and if possible, adventurous occupation. Meanwhile,
he now bethought him of a desire he had long had, to take
to himself a life partner, in the person of some young and
noble-born Venetian lady. Before leaving Cathay, he had
told his father that, on their return, he would marry, and
thus perpetuate the name and wealth of the family; and now

seemed a favorable time to put this design into execution.

He began to look about him with a view to selecting some fair companion. There were many beauties at the Venetian court, and a man of Marco's handsome, manly appearance and great fame might be sure of a favorable hearing, to whichever of them he chose to address himself.

But before he had been able to make his choice amid such a bevy of pretty women, an event occurred which drew him away, for a time, from all thoughts of marriage. During the year before the return of the Polos from the East, a fierce war had broken out between Venice and her ancient and bitter rival, the city of Genoa. These two cities, both boasting of a most thriving commerce, and both powerful and warlike, had long contested with each other the supremacy of the seas. Nearly a hundred years before, Venice had performed the feat of capturing Constantinople, and had thus won the alliance of the Eastern Roman Empire. After that period, both Venice and Genoa had established many colonies in the Levant, on the shores of Asia Minor and Greece, and on the islands that dotted the Aegean. Fifty years after the taking of Constantinople by Venice, a fierce war had broken out between her and Genoa, in Asia Minor, resulting in a brilliant triumph by Venice. Then came a time when Genoa in turn was victorious, and drove her rival from many places which Venice had taken from her.

The new war, begun in 1294, when Marco and his party were sailing on the Indian ocean, homeward bound, had at first been favorable to the Genoese, who had defeated the

Venetians in a great sea battle off the coast of Palestine, taking almost their entire fleet; and this war was still going on when Marco returned to Venice.

News had now come that the Genoese had fitted out a formidable squadron, and were resolved to attack the proud old city of Venice itself. They had won so many victories, that they arrogantly believed that, by a great effort, they might capture even the famed capital of the doges. The news of this approaching peril filled Venice with excitement and fury. The haughty Venetians were beside themselves with rage to think that so audacious a plan should be thought of by their ancient foes; and every preparation was made in all haste to give them a hot reception.

The doge called upon every Venetian cavalier to aid in saving their beloved city from a crowning disgrace; and his call was promptly obeyed by all the flower of Venetian chivalry. Marco Polo's heart was fired with patriotic ardor among the foremost. He saw with delight a chance to return to a life of action and peril, and to win new laurels by his prowess; and he was one of the first to offer his sword and his life to the doge. No sooner had he done so, than he was appointed to the command of one of the galleys in the fleet which was being rapidly prepared to resist that of the Genoese.

The enemy's expedition, comprising nearly one hundred war galleys, was commanded by a famous admiral, named Doria. Soon the news reached Venice that this fleet had assembled at the Gulf of Spezia, near Genoa, and had thence set sail around the Italian peninsula for the Adriatic. Then couriers arrived with the startling intelligence that the Genoese galleys were actually in the Adriatic, and were rapidly approaching Venice itself.

But at this moment the elements served as the ally of the Venetians. A furious storm of wind and rain broke over the Genoese fleet; Doria hastened to put into a port on the Dalmatian coast, with such galleys as he could gather; while some sixteen of his galleys were swept far away from him by the tempest.

When the storm abated, Doria was forced to pursue his design with about eighty galleys. After ravaging the Dalmatian coast, the greater part of which belonged to Venice, the Genoese advanced to the island of Curzola, the same that the ancient Greeks called Corcyra. Here he put in at the harbor of the chief town, which, as it belonged to the Venetians, Doria ruthlessly sacked and burned. All these events were learned by the doge soon after they had occurred; and now a Venetian fleet had been collected, comprising ninety-five galleys, and put under the command of a veteran sea-warrior named Dandolo.

The Genoese fleet were riding confidently at anchor in the bay of Curzola, when, one hazy afternoon in early September, they perceived the Venetian galleys in close ranks, approaching from the southern side of the island. They came to anchor in sight of the Genoese, and the sun went down upon the two fleets confronting each other, and only waiting for the morning light to engage in a deadly conflict. STOP

Both sides were very sure of victory. After the night

had fallen Doria, the Genoese admiral, called a council of war, and put the question whether they should attack the enemy in the morning, or stand on the defensive and await his assault where they were. It was decided to attack. At the same time the Venetian commander, Dandolo, was so confident of beating the Genoese, that he was sending out boats to watch that the Genoese did not sneak away under cover of night. Marco Polo was in command of his galley in Dandolo's fleet; and no warrior in it was more passionately eager than he for the fray.

The sun rose bright and clear on the next morning, which was a Sunday. From earliest dawn the greatest activity prevailed in both fleets. The long galleys, with their multitudes of slim oars, their many flags flying and fluttering in the fresh breeze, their warriors, with shield, sword and lance, crowded not only on the deck, but on platforms raised above it, and in basket-like boxes hoisted nearly to the tops of the masts, their trumpeters blowing martial blasts in raised enclosures near the stern, their captains shouting hoarsely the words of command, presented a gay and bold appearance as they advanced to meet the foe. Marco's galley was one of the largest and best-manned in Dandolo's fleet; and as the vessels sped forward, was one of those which led the way.

The Genoese had resolved to make the attack; but to their surprise, the Venetians appeared coming down upon them the first thing in the morning. The Venetian galleys had full sail on, for the wind was in their favor. On the other hand, as they were proceeding eastward, the sun shone directly in their eyes. The air was filled with the noise of their trumpets and the shouting of the warriors; and there was a moment when Doria, seeing his enemy's brave array and bold advance, trembled lest they should overcome him.

The first shock of the battle seemed to give reason to his fears. The Venetian galleys came on with an impetuous rush, and plunged pell-mell among those of Genoa. Before Doria was able to make a single stroke, no less than ten of his galleys had been captured and sunk, Marco Polo having been one of the capturers. But the Venetians had advanced too rapidly, as the event soon showed; for scarcely had Dandolo heard with joy of the taking of the ten galleys, when word came to him that several of his own boats had run aground. This was a great misfortune. It was soon to be followed by the capture of one of his largest galleys, the soldiers in which were thrown by the Genoese into the water; and the galley itself was turned against Dandolo. The tide of battle, raging fiercely, had seemed at first to run decidedly in favor of the Venetians. But now it turned. The Venetians became confused and desperate by these mishaps; while the Genoese were filled with new hope and courage. Nevertheless, the conflict went on desperately for hours, victory inclining now to one side and now to the other.

Marco, with his galley, fought like a lion. He stood on a platform above his men, and kept encouraging them by his shouts and his own example. Every now and then, fired by the excitement of the fray, he would descend from the

Marco Polo in Battle

platform, and drawing his long sword, would rush into the midst, and rain sturdy blows upon the heads of the Genoese in reach of it.

The contest had gone on till the sun was far in the west, when the Genoese fleet, rallying together for a desperate rush, formed a close rank of galleys, and plunged straight down upon Dandolo's boats. So impetuous was the assault that it scattered the Venetian galleys right and left. At this critical moment, an event occurred that completed the defeat and destruction of the brave Venetians. Sixteen Genoese galleys, which had been driven away from the rest of the Genoese fleet, in the storm which had assailed it on entering the Adriatic, now came up, and fell upon the Venetian vessels with crushing force.

This decided the battle. Venetian galleys, one after another, were sunk or captured, the men resisting heroically to the last; until nearly every galley which still floated fell into the hands of the victorious Genoese. A few escaped, and made all sail for Venice; but among the captive vessels was the admiral's ship, in which Dandolo himself was taken.

One of the very last galleys to yield to the conqueror was that of Marco Polo. He contested every inch with the foe, and it was only after his masts had gone, his men had been dreadfully thinned out, and all the other Venetian galleys around him had fallen into the hands of the Genoese, that he sadly surrendered and shared the humiliating fate of his brave commander.

The prisoners were all taken into port, where they were forced to witness the exultant rejoicing of their enemies.

The commanders of the captured galleys were confined in a house together, and Marco found himself in company with Dandolo. The Venetian admiral was overwhelmed with grief at his defeat. In spite of the entreaties of his guard and of Marco himself, Dandolo utterly refused to take any food; and one day, in utter despair, he threw himself down, violently struck his head against a bench, and thus killed himself. He preferred to die thus, rather than be carried a prisoner to hated Genoa.

Doria heard with grief of the violent death of his gallant enemy, and ordered that Dandolo's body should be embalmed and carried to Genoa, where a funeral worthy of his fame should be given him. Having rested his army and repaired his galleys, Doria, ordering his prisoners to be chained and put on board, set sail for his own city.

This was a dreary moment, indeed, for Marco; a sad ending to his ambition for military glory. Instead of returning home bearing the honors of his prowess, he was a captive, loaded with chains, and on the way to prison in a strange and hostile country. Here was a sorrowful termination to his plans of marriage, and his hope of sitting in the midst of a family of blooming children. Instead of his luxurious home in the Court of the Millions, a bare dark cell was destined to be his lot. But he bore up bravely in the midst of his misfortunes. His nature was so cheerful a one, that instead of brooding, he tried to encourage and enliven his fellow prisoners; and won the liking of the Genoese soldiers whose duty it was to guard and serve him.

In due time the victorious fleet reached Genoa, and

was received with the wildest demonstrations of delight.
The ships in the beautiful bay displayed their flags and
banners; the great nobles vied with each other in paying
honor to Doria; and a splendid funeral was awarded to the
dead Venetian admiral. The prisoners, still in chains, were
marched through the streets, bounded on either side by
stately palaces, and were jeered at by the multitude as they
passed along. Finally, to Marco's great relief, they reached
a massive and gloomy edifice, not far from the quays, into
which they were taken, and distributed in narrow cells.

For some time, at first, Marco feared that his captors had
doomed him to all the horrors of solitary imprisonment. He
was aghast at the idea of spending months, perhaps years,
shut up in darkness and dampness, utterly alone, with no
companion, however humble, to share his solitude. He was
greatly relieved, therefore, when one day after he had been
in prison about a week, the governor of the jail entered his
cell, followed by a grave, scholarly-looking man, to whom
the governor introduced Marco as his future prison-mate.

As soon as the governor had retired, Marco rushed
forward and grasped the new-comer by the hand, eagerly
asking him who he was and whence he came.

"I am Rustician, a gentleman of Pisa," replied the stranger;
"and was taken prisoner by the Genoese several years ago.
Ever since, I have languished in one prison or another; but
now, since such large numbers of you Venetians have been
taken, the prisons of Genoa are full, and they are obliged
to put two men in each cell. And who, pray, are you?"

Marco told the Pisan who he was, and gave him a full

account of his wanderings; and speedily they found themselves fast friends.

The Pisan proved to a be scholar and writer of rare accomplishments, and he, in turn, was delighted to find, in his fellow-prisoner, a man who had seen so much of a continent almost wholly unknown to Europeans. The companionship of Rustician, indeed, made Marco's prison life almost cheerful. They talked to each other by the hour, Marco listening to Rustician's learned conversation, and Rustician eagerly absorbing Marco's stories of the marvels of the East. Meanwhile, the severity of their prison life was gradually relaxed, until at last they were allowed comfortable couches to sleep on, and an abundance of palatable food at their daily meals.

The prison was a large one, and contained several hundred prisoners; these were for the most part Venetians who, like Marco, had been taken in the battle of Curzola. After a time, the prisoners were allowed to see and talk with each other at certain hours of the day; a permission of which Marco eagerly availed himself. He found many of his friends among the prisoners, as well as a number of the men who had served on board his own galley. Among other privileges which were now allowed the captives, were those of having books and writing materials in their cells, and of writing to and receiving letters from their friends at home; and Marco took good care to send his father a full account of all that happened to him in prison.

But his chief pleasure was to talk with his roommate, the gentle and learned Rustician. They had speedily become close and loving friends; and Rustician, as soon as they were allowed pen and ink, bethought him of a way to pass the weary hours, for which the world owes him a deep debt of gratitude. He proposed to Marco that he should sit down day after day, and relate, in due order, all his travels and what befell him in the East, describing the countries and peoples he had seen, and the many adventures which had happened to him; while Rustician himself, sitting at the little prison table, should carefully write off Marco's thrilling story. To this Marco readily consented; and the next day the two captives set to work upon their new labor in good earnest.

CHAPTER XVII.

MARCO POLO A PRISONER

5/15

ARCO Polo had accepted Rusticiano's proposition, to dictate to him an account of his travels, with pleasure. It afforded a grateful relief from the monotony of prison life; and, besides, Marco well knew that the wonderful narrative would perpetuate his fame long after he himself was dead.

We may picture to ourselves the two men, seated on the rude chairs of their cell; Marco leaning against the wall, and leisurely recounting his adventures, while the grave Rusticiano slowly wrote at the table. Sometimes the scholar would stop, and look at Marco with incredulous amazement, as he related some story that seemed to Rusticiano beyond belief; but Marco would nod his head emphatically, and assert that what he told was not half the truth. Then Rusticiano would quietly shrug his shoulders, and go on writing.

Thus sped quickly the hours, days, and weeks. The imprisonment of both seemed the shorter for this pleasant labor; and Rusticiano was very careful, when the day's work was over, to deposit the precious manuscript where it would be safe.

Meanwhile, the rules of the prison were gradually relaxed in Marco's favor. He was allowed to roam about the gloomy old edifice pretty much as he pleased, and to take ample exercise in the courtyard. Gradually it became known in Genoa and the country round about, that a famous Venetian traveller occupied the prison, and then Marco began to receive many visits from the principal personages of the city. Crowds gathered at the prison gate to catch a glimpse of him; dames of noble rank sent him presents of books and rare wines. The carriages of noblemen jostled each other at the prison gates, as their occupants waited for an opportunity of talking with the traveller. The governor of the prison invited Marco and his companion Rusticiano, to dine at his table; and finally, they were transferred to another cell which was large, well lighted and ventilated, and handsomely and luxuriously furnished; while the food placed before them was as rich and various as that supplied to a nobleman's family.

The prisoners now lived in the greatest comfort. The walls were lined with book shelves; they slept on soft couches at night; and, had it not been for the heavy bars across the windows, they would have scarcely known that they were prisoners at all. Every day their apartment—for it could no longer be called a cell—was thronged with visitors; and every little while Marco gave dinners and suppers to his visitors, and made very merry with them. Months thus passed, not wholly without their pleasures and consolations. But Marco often grieved at his situation, and became impatient to regain his freedom. It seemed cruel that, no sooner had he found himself at home after his long sojourn in the east, he should have been captured and doomed to suffer exile and the grim slavery of dungeon walls. He longed to breathe once more the free air of Venice, to settle down among his kindred, and to reap the reward of all his toils, in the establishment of a family and the enjoyment of his well-earned riches. Yet there seemed no prospect of his captivity coming to an end. He knew that Venetians were often kept prisoners at Genoa for many years, and he saw no reason to hope that he would be set at liberty sooner than the rest.

One day, after he had been at Genoa about five months, Marco was sitting at his table with Rusticiano, reading, when the door of his room was thrown open, and two men entered. At first Marco did not recognize them; but when one of them advanced, and took off his cap, he saw that it was his father, Nicolo, and that his companion was Marco's brother, Maffeo. In a moment Marco was locked in his father's close embrace. The emotion of all three at meeting was so great, that for a while neither could speak. At last Marco exclaimed:

"You have filled me with joy, father and brother, by coming to me! How did you venture into the territory of our enemies?"

"I could bear no longer the thought of your imprisonment," answered Nicolo, wiping his eyes; "and so I sought and procured the consent of the Genoese to come hither, and see you, my dear son, and to try to obtain your liberty."

"Alas, father," returned Marco, shaking his head mournfully, "I fear it will be of no avail. The Genoese treat me with the most generous kindness, but they have no idea of setting me free."

Nicolo groaned as he heard these words; but Maffeo with cheerful voice, said, "Do not despair, father. We come with the offer of a heavy ransom. Perhaps the Genoese will yield to a golden argument."

"We can but try," replied Nicolo. Then all three sat down, and began to talk of all that had happened to them since the time they had parted at Venice. Marco told his father and brother the history of his prison life, the indulgence shown him by his captors, and the consolation he had had in the friendship of the learned and warm-hearted Rusticiano. Of home news that Nicolo gave him in return, there was little that was interesting. This friend had married and that friend had died, but the course of life at their own home had gone smoothly on. Marco observed that his father was more bent, gray and feeble than when he had seen him last; and knew that grief at his own misfortunes was, in part at least, the cause of Nicolo's altered appearance.

The effort to secure his liberty proved, as Marco had predicted, unsuccessful. In vain Nicolo offered the Genoese a large sum as a ransom they refused to think of setting Marco free. But Nicolo at least procured one privilege for his son. The government consented that Marco should be released from prison and live as he pleased in the city, on condition that he would give his word of honor that he would not attempt to escape from it.

Nicolo hastened to the prison with the news of this

fresh favor, and Marco was delighted at least to bid adieu to the gloomy walls which had so long confined him. His effects were soon packed, and he took up his residence in one of the best inns in Genoa. He parted from Rusticiano with much regret, and promised that he would come to the prison very often and see him, and would try to procure the same favor for his friend that he himself had just secured. This he soon after succeeded in accomplishing.

It was with keen sorrow that Marco parted from his father and brother. It seemed very doubtful whether he should ever see Nicolo again; he himself might be kept at Genoa for the rest of his life, and he felt very unhappy to be left behind, while his father and brother were free to return to Venice.

But in his new situation Marco soon recovered his buoyant spirits. No longer treated as a prisoner, he lived like a Genoese gentleman, and had as his friends and companions men of wealth and rank. Wherever he went he was treated with great honor and respect. He was invited to all the fashionable balls and fetes, and often attended them; and with his ample means, was able to indulge his desires and tastes as he pleased.

It has already been said that, before leaving the court of the great khan, Marco had made up his mind that on reaching home, he would marry, and rear a family of children. His departure for the war had postponed the execution of this design, and now there seemed no prospect that he could carry it out. He desired to perpetuate his name, family, and property; yet now, when he was over forty years old, he found himself still a bachelor.

But though Marco could not, situated as he was, think of marriage, his father Nicolo had not experienced the same difficulty; for, old as he was, Nicolo, some time before Marco had been taken prisoner, had taken to himself a new wife. Marco's new step-mother was considerably younger than himself; and he was rejoiced to think that now, in all probability, the family name and fame was in no danger of dying out.

In course of time the news came to him of the birth of a little step-brother and Marco was greatly amused to think of being the brother at over forty, of a little fellow just come into the world. Then he heard the sad intelligence that his father Nicolo had suddenly died, leaving his young widow and child. Marco grieved much that he could not have been at the old man's bedside in his last hours. He sent word to Venice that a splendid tomb should be erected in Nicolo's honored memory, in the Church of San Lorenzo, at his own expense. This tomb, consisting of a sarcophagus of solid stone, upon which was engraved the coat-of-arms of the Polos, long stood under the portico of that venerable edifice. STOP

5/16 The quarrel between Venice and Genoa, which had now lasted for many years, and still continued, was the cause why Marco and his comrades in the war were yet retained as prisoners. Many attempts had been made to bring about peace between the rival cities, each of whom proudly claimed to be queen of the sea. After Marco had been at Genoa about a year, he heard one day with great delight that the Prince of Milan had become a mediator between the two foes, and was making every effort to induce them to come to terms. Both Venice and Genoa, indeed, were tired of the long strife, which had not resulted in any very important gain on either side; and the Prince of Milan did not find it very difficult to make them listen to reason. Envoys from Venice and Genoa went to Milan, and after they had talked the matter over with each other, finally agreed upon terms of peace. Among these terms were, that when the treaty was signed the prisoners on both sides should be released and returned to their homes. In due time the news came that the doge of Venice and duke of Genoa had both signed the treaty, and that the two cities were friends again.

Marco was entertaining a number of friends at supper when it was announced to him that he was at last free to return to Venice. Among his guests were some Venetians, who like himself were prisoners, and who had been allowed to reside outside the prison walls. These rose from the table and, with tears in their eyes, embraced each other and Marco. The Genoese gentlemen who were present exclaimed that now the Venetians were their brothers, and a scene of great hilarity and rejoicing followed, and was continued far into the night.

But Marco, though free, was not allowed to depart at once. His many Genoese friends, who had already become strongly attached to him, insisted that he should attend the banquets and fetes which were to celebrate the return of peace, and some of which were to be given in his own honor. The duke of Genoa invited all the high nobility of the "City of Palaces" to his own palace, where night was turned into day by gorgeous illuminations, and from whose towers floated the flags of the sister cities between whom concord once more reigned. Among the brilliant throng, Marco's stalwart form and handsome face were conspicuous, and everywhere he went he was surrounded by admiring groups. The duke himself invited Marco to walk beside him to the banqueting hall, where he was placed at the sovereign's right hand. At the dukes fete, too, were very many of the gallant Venetians who had fought with Marco at Curzola, and had since shared his captivity.

Now that friendship was restored between the two cities, the Genoese were resolved to treat their late prisoners with all honor and attention. A fleet of galleys was ordered to anchor in the picturesque bay, for the purpose of transporting the Venetians home. These were fitted up with every luxury and comfort, that the voyage might be as pleasant as possible; and a store of provisions was stored away in them, comprising good things enough to supply the travellers with bounteous meals throughout the transit.

Before Marco took his departure, he paid a visit to his old prison comrade, the worthy Rusticiano. Rusticiano was still a prisoner, though Genoa had just made peace with Pisa, and he was looking forward to a speedy release. The interview between the two friends was therefore a very happy one; and Marco made Rusticiano promise that, ere long, he would pay him a visit in Venice.

On a hot morning in the midsummer of 1299, the Venetians embarked on the galleys, homeward bound. A vast crowd of Genoese thronged the quays to see them off and bid them God speed on their voyage. Marco, on reaching the scene of departure, was almost suffocated by the warm reception given him by his Genoese friends. They pressed close around him and embraced him, and would scarcely let him go to proceed on board his galley.

At last he found himself standing upon the deck, and gazing for the last time at the noble and stately city which had dealt so gently with him as a captive, and where, in spite of his captivity, he had formed so many pleasant ties and passed so many happy hours. The signal was given; the fleet of galleys, gay with flags and pennons, and alive with the quick movements of the many long oars, glided away from the quays; the multitude on shore gave a great shout of farewell, the Genoese ladies waving their veils, and the men their plumed hats; and soon the vineclad eminences and long lines of palaces disappeared from view.

Meanwhile word had gone to Venice that the prisoners had been released, and were on their way home by sea. Immediately the city was thrown into a great commotion. It was resolved that the heroes of Curzola should have a reception worthy of their bravery and their misfortunes; and every preparation was made to greet them with the most distinguished honors. Among the prisoners, who numbered more than a thousand, were many Venetian youths of noble birth, the hopes of haughty houses, the beloved of many a fair damsel of rank and beauty. It seemed, indeed, as if there were scarcely a noble family in Venice who had not been bereft of a son in the heroic but disastrous sea-fight.

Had there been powder in these times, no doubt the cannon would have boomed forth a deafening roar of boisterous welcome as, on the misty August afternoon, the fleet of Genoese galleys made its appearance in the Gulf of Venice. As it was, the whole city seemed fluttering with flags and banners; from the doge's palace and the lofty Campanile, from the Byzantine domes and pinacles of St. Mark's, from the spires of churches and the summits of bell towers, waved innumerable standards, bearing the national device of the winged lion. Towards the quays, every balcony of the ducal palace and the council houses, the palaces of the proud nobles of Venice, and the terraces on the edge of the grand canal, were thronged with a gay and excited multitude. The doge himself, with his long, pointed cap, his rich robes sweeping the ground, and his white beard flowing over his breast, stood, surrounded by his brilliant court, on the quay in front of his palace; while on every side of the square was drawn up the flower of the Venetian army, the lancers and crossbowmen being conspicuous. In the bay and canal, countless gondolas awaited the arrival. As the fleet of galleys came nearer, they were greeted by the long and loud applause of the multitude on shore; and it was with difficulty that the soldiers prevented the crowd from invading the quay where the prisoners were to land. At last the galleys were safely moored. The oarsmen raised their oars, and held them upright in long lines along the decks. Then the prisoners, in groups of twos and threes, advanced up the planks, and sprang on shore. First they advanced to the doge, who welcomed them with cordial words of affection and praise. Then each sought his parents, sweethearts or friends, in the swaying crowd or on the overflowing balconies.

Marco soon found himself in the arms of his brother and uncle, while other relatives and friends huddled excitedly around him. They talked to each other rapidly and earnestly; and as soon as they could make their way through the crowd, they hastened across the square of St. Mark, and taking a gondola, were soon speeding towards the street of San Giovanni Chrysostomo. The retainers of the household were waiting in a group in front of the "Court of the Millions" to welcome their master home; and as he landed from the gondola, formed in a line on either side, and bowed low while he passed, with brother and friends, through the archway.

That night, as may well be believed, there were sounds of revelry and rejoicing in the spacious mansion of the Polos. Marco thought of his return, with his father and uncle, from Cathay; and could not restrain himself from shedding a tear when he saw his father's vacant seat at the groaning board. He was now to take the old man's place; his voyages, travels and adventures over, he would henceforth live quietly at home, and devote himself to the service of his family and of the state, reaping the reward of the perils he had passed and the fame he had won.

CHAPTER XVIII.

LAST DAYS OF MARCO POLO

T the time of Marco Polo's return to Venice, he was about forty-six years old, that is, in the prime of manhood. He might yet look forward to many years of health and vigor; and might, had he so chosen, have undertaken new expeditions to remote lands. But he had at last grown tired of wandering. In his prison life at Genoa, he had often thought how happy he might be in a home of his own, with a loving wife by his side, and children playing about his knees; and had felt that with such a home he would be quite content to settle down for the rest of his life.

On finding himself at Venice once more, he arranged his affairs as if he were now resolved to settle down there. He fitted up his house anew; and now for the first time took part in the affairs of commerce which his family had long pursued. He owned a large share in the trade which they carried on; and soon was busily engaged as a merchant.

Then he began to look about him for a wife. As a nobleman and a traveller of the greatest distinction, Marco Polo was a welcome guest in the best houses in Venice. He was invited everywhere, and, had he chosen, he might have gone every night to some feast or ball. His friends were countless, and belonged to the highest social rank; while his own hospitable nature continually filled his house with merry parties, gay masqueraders, and hilarious feasters. His tall, stalwart person, his courteous bearing, his fine, expressive features, and his wide renown, made him a special favorite with the noble dames and demoiselles of Venice, who loved to hear him recount his adventures, and showed him, in many coquettish ways, their admiration of his exploits. To them he was a brave hero, who had fearlessly encountered many perils, and had survived the most bitter hardships and hairbreadth escapes.

Marco therefore had ample opportunities to make choice of a life partner; it seemed certain that wherever he paid his court, he was sure of being kindly received.

Among the noble families whose acquaintance he had made after his return from Cathay, was that of the Loredanos. The head of the family was a wealthy nobleman, a member of the doge's council, and a man of mark in Venice. Loredano had two lovely daughters. One, Donata, was a tall, stately brunette, about twenty-five; the younger, Maria, was a delicate blonde, with rich auburn hair. Marco Polo was soon attracted to the beauty and graces of Donata. To be sure, he was twenty years older than she; but his heart was still fresh and young, and had never before been touched by the passion of love. It was all the stronger in a man of his age and vigor. He soon became very attentive to the young signorita. He visited her at her father's house, or in her company sped over the beautiful bay in his luxurious gondola. It was observed that he was always at her side at the balls and fetes, and that he paid her special honor at the festivities at which she was present in his own house.

The fair Donata seemed pleased with his attentions, and gradually learned to feel for the sturdy cavalier a warm affection. The course of their love ran smooth; and when Marco Polo asked the consent of Loredano to their betrothal, the noble councillor at once and joyfully accorded it.

Then came sweet, happy days when the middle-aged cavalier courted his young lady love, and spent long dreamy hours in her beloved company. Never a day passed that he did not spend a portion of it with her. It soon became known through Venice that Marco Polo was to wed Donata Loredano; and their friends vied with each other in giving parties and masques in honor of the event.

This pleasant courtship was not of long duration, for Marco was eager to be "married and settled." The wedding was a grand affair. It took place in the stately church of San Lorenzo, where Nicolo Polo lay buried, and which was destined also to receive the remains of his more famous son. The ceremony was performed by an archbishop, assisted by numerous priests. The doge with all his retinue was there, and so was the flower of the nobility and wealth of Venice.

The bridegroom, attended by his brother and other relatives, made his appearance in a gorgeous suit of satin, while about his neck hung a massive chain of gold, the insignia of a knightly order which had been conferred upon him. Upon his head he wore a satin cap, above which rose several flowing feathers of white and blue; while at his side hung a jewelled scimitar, which had been given to him by Kublai Khan as a token of his affection. The multitudes that crowded densely the sombre old church noted the manly presence, the proud carriage, and the noble features of Marco Polo, as he strode up the nave beneath the high, echoing arches, and declared to themselves that even at his age, he made a comely and imposing bridegroom.

The bride appeared splendidly dressed, with a long gauzy veil that flowed to her feet, and every part of her dress sparkling with jewels. She looked beautiful and happy, and all the world envied Marco Polo his possession of the fair Donata Loredano.

The wedding festivities lasted, as was the custom in Venice, a week. They began with a bounteous banquet at the Court of the Millions, which was kept up till the streaks of dawn shot between the heavily curtained windows. There were fetes of gondolas on the water, sports at a country seat which Marco Polo had purchased out of his abundant wealth, and masquerades at the palaces of Loredano and other friends. STOP

5|18 Then followed the quietest and perhaps the pleasantest period of Marco Polo's life. Established in his luxurious home at the Court of the Millions, surrounded by hosts of friends who were devotedly attached to him, with a lovely wife whom he adored and who admired and loved him, held in high esteem and confidence by the doge and all the highest dignitaries of the Republic, abundantly able to indulge in every pleasure and recreation for which his taste inclined him, his lot indeed seemed a fortunate one.

There was plenty of work to occupy his time in the business house which had so long been carried on by his family, and which was still in a prosperous condition. In this he took a keen personal interest, and thus at once employed his time profitably, and added new stores to his abundant wealth. His travels in the East had been of great benefit to the trade of his house; for he had made the acquaintance of many merchants in Persia, India, Arabia, Asia Minor, and Constantinople, and had formed business connections with them which were now of much advantage to his trade.

Not long after he had married and settled, Marco Polo was surprised and delighted to receive a visit from two Persian travellers of high rank, who had come to Venice on a commercial errand. They went to the Court of the Millions to see Marco, of whose fame as a traveller they had heard, and to bear him a message of friendship from the fair young queen Cocachin, who gratefully remembered Marco's gallant attentions to her while journeying from Cathay to Persia, and who sent him a beautiful jewel in token of her gratitude. Marco was grieved to learn, about a year afterwards, that this lovely young queen had died, mourned by all her new subjects and by her gallant husband.

Marco soon found himself one of the most important citizens of Venice. Still active and energetic, he began to take part in public affairs; and ere very long, was chosen by the doge a member of his grand council, in which he soon won the reputation of being a sagacious and keen-sighted statesman. There was a time, indeed, when it seemed not unlikely that the great traveller might some day be himself elected doge; but the prospect passed away before his death. Meanwhile, he not only served the state as councillor, but went on embassies to various countries, and made treaties of peace or alliance, and patched up quarrels.

In due time, Marco Polo found himself the father of a thriving young family. Three little daughters were the fruit of his union with his beloved Donata—Fantina, Bellela, and Moreta. They grew up to be as pretty and gentle as their names. Marco greatly desired to have a son, who should be the heir of his name and wealth. But Providence denied him this blessing. He was delighted with his little girls, however, and when they became old enough, was wont to take them on his knee, and relate to them the strange adventures he had met with by land and sea in remote lands. They were very proud of their father, who had seen and done such wonderful things; and listened as eagerly to his stories as children do nowadays to the Arabian Nights and Robinson Crusoe.

As the girls grew up, they proved as handsome and engaging as their mother had been in her own youth; and now the Court of the Millions was besieged by gallant young suitors for their hands. There was not a youth in Venice who would not have been proud to ally himself to so distinguished a family as that of the Polos had become; and such was the beauty of Fantina and Bellela, that had they been poor, they would not have lacked ardent wooers. Then other weddings were celebrated at the Court of the Millions. Fantina first, and then Bellela, chose their cavaliers, and were duly wedded to them; and Marco Polo, now wrinkled and grizzled, was soon happy to find himself a grandfather. Thus many years passed in serene and contented prosperity. Marco, as he grew older, was less and less tempted to attempt new adventures. He was blessed with a delightful home, was crowned with plenteous honors, and felt himself a conspicuous personage of the time. He was often visited by travellers from a distance, both from Western Europe and from the more remote East; and always received them with the bounteous hospitality for which he was known far and wide.

He lived nearly a quarter of a century after his return from captivity at Genoa; and rose bright and well on the morn of his seventieth birthday, appearing as if he had yet many years to survive. But soon after, he was laid low by a fever which from the first betrayed serious symptoms that alarmed his family. He grew worse and worse; and the news spread through Venice that the illustrious Marco Polo lay dangerously ill.

Immediately the doors of the Court of the Millions were besieged by crowds of anxious and inquiring friends. The doge sent daily to ask after the health of his honored councillor; and Marco's wife and daughters tended at the bedside night and day. It soon became but too apparent that the life of the heroic old traveller was fast ebbing away. Still his mind was often clear, and then he talked serenely and even cheerfully with his beloved ones. He had always been good and upright, and death, which he had so often braved in years gone by, had but few terrors for him now. Then came a sad day when the doctors despaired of restoring him to health, and gently broke the news to the grief-stricken wife and daughters. Marco Polo still lingered a few days, growing feebler and feebler each hour, but suffering little pain. One sunny morning, the end came. It was peaceful, serene, and happy as his later life had been. The old man sank gently into Donata's arms, and ceased to breathe.

Venice was wrapt in gloom at the death of its most famous citizen; and for several days no other subject was talked of in its marts and in the public squares where the people met to chat and gossip. The doge and his court went into mourning, and tributes to Marco Polo's memory were paid in the grand council of the Republic. He was buried with great pomp and ceremony, and laid in the old church of San Lorenza beside his good father, and where his own marriage, and the christening and marriage of his elder daughters, had taken place.

His memory was kept green by the Venetians for generations and centuries after his death. Three hundred years after, a stately marble statue of him was erected by the city in one of its squares, and still stands to commemorate the honor in which Venice held him; while, two centuries after his death, his direct descendant, Trevesano, was elected doge, and presided over the Republic.

Thus lived, and thus died at the goodly age of three-score and ten, the greatest of the early explorers of the remote and unknown regions of the Orient; who may be said to have introduced Europe and Asia to each other, and to have discovered the vast possibilities of a commerce between the two continents. He thus did invaluable service to the world; and it is pleasant to remember that, after all the perils and vicissitudes through which he passed, the long and weary exile from home that he suffered, and the subsequent misfortune he encountered while fighting for the preservation of Venice, he reaped the full reward of his perseverance and patriotism, and enjoyed a long after-life of prosperity, honor, happiness and domestic bliss; and that his memory still lives, his name being written high up on the roll of the world's most illustrious discoverers and benefactors.

THE END.

Made in United States
North Haven, CT
05 August 2022

22332192R00136